Teaching to Avoid Plagiarism

Teaching to Avoid Plagiarism

How to promote good source use

Diane Pecorari

Open University Press

Open University Press
McGraw-Hill Education
McGraw-Hill House
Shoppenhangers Road
Maidenhead
Berkshire
England
SL6 2QL

email: enquiries@openup.co.uk
world wide web: www.openup.co.uk

and Two Penn Plaza, New York, NY 10121-2289, USA

First published 2013

A catalogue record of this book is available from the British Library

ISBN-13: 978-0-33-524593-2 (pb)
ISBN-10: 0-33-524593-5 (pb)
eISBN: 978-0-33-524594-9

Library of Congress Cataloging-in-Publication Data
CIP data applied for

Typesetting and e-book compilations by
RefineCatch Limited, Bungay, Suffolk

Praise for this book

"*Diane Pecorari's book provides practical examples and activities on handling plagiarism blended with research-based findings. It is useful for teachers wanting to improve their understanding and practices in managing plagiarism, but also student advisors and academic support skills staff who deal with issues of academic integrity. This book makes a unique contribution to the field of plagiarism management as its structure affords direct professional development opportunities. Assessment tasks, broad questions and activities are provided at the end of each chapter, encouraging readers to understand both policy and practice in their own institution to better manage plagiarism and source attribution.* "

Dr Wendy Sutherland-Smith, School of Psychology, Faculty of Health, Deakin University, Australia

"*Teaching to Avoid Plagiarism successfully turns attention away from the detection and punishment of plagiarism and focuses instead on understanding and prevention through the promotion of good source use. Combining practical activities based on real-life examples with wide-ranging original research, this important book should be required reading, not only for staff development officers and lecturers, but more widely throughout the higher education community.*"

Maggie Charles, Oxford University Language Centre

"*Diane Pecorari's insightful research and scholarship on plagiarism is used to excellent effect in this book which advocates a proactive rather than reactive approach to the difficulties faced by students in learning how to integrate their source texts. Thoughtful activities and discussion questions aimed at staff development are teamed with advice on ways to build in support within disciplinary writing which will help students master the necessary academic skills to avoid plagiarism. The emphasis, quite rightly, is also on helping students understand how plagiarism disrupts the ethical values of the academy, and is not just another hurdle placed in their way by academic insiders.*"

Dr Ann Hewings, Director, Centre for Language and Communication, The Open University

"*As stated by Diane Pecorari in the first sentence of this excellent volume, 'plagiarism is a problem in our universities'. The volume demonstrates clearly how teachers and students can deal with this 'problem' by developing a better understanding of the phenomenon, on the one hand, and developing specific skills in dealing with it, on the other. Working from the principle that 'an ounce of prevention is worth a pound of cure', Diane Pecorari argues for a proactive approach to handling issues of plagiarism, with an emphasis on the need to train students how to deal appropriately with sources. As well as a clear exposition of the theoretical issues at stake, the book contains a wealth of practical activities and discussion questions which will allow readers to develop the sort of competence in dealing with plagiarism that is the goal of the volume.*"

Professor John Flowerdew, City University of Hong Kong

For Jeff, who helped in so many ways

Thank you for shopping at Amazon.co.uk!

Invoice for
Your order of 6 September, 2013
Order ID 203-9068499-8935556
Invoice number D3MV0GTJR
Invoice date 6 September, 2013

Billing Address
Anne Haig Smith
Abingdon & Witney College
Holloway Road
Witney, Oxon OX28 6NE
United Kingdom

Shipping Address
Anne Haig Smith
Abingdon And Witney College
Wootton Road
ABINGDON, Oxon OX14 1GG
United Kingdom

Qty.	Item	Our Price (excl. VAT)	VAT Rate	Total Price
1	**Teaching to Avoid Plagiarism** Paperback. Pecorari, Diane. 0335245935 (** P 2-F61E104 **)	£24.99	0%	£24.99
	Shipping charges	£0.00		£0.00
	Subtotal (excl. VAT) 0%			£24.99
	Total VAT			£0.00
	Total			£24.99

Conversion rate - £1.00 : EUR 1,19

This shipment completes your order.

You can always check the status of your orders or change your account details from the 'Your Account' link at the top of each page on our site.

Thinking of returning an item? PLEASE USE OUR ON-LINE RETURNS SUPPORT CENTRE.

Our Returns Support Centre (www.amazon.co.uk/returns-support) will guide you through our Returns Policy and provide you with a printable personalised return label. Please have your order number ready (you can find it next to your order summary, above). Our Returns Policy does not affect your statutory rights.

Amazon EU S.a.r.L, 5 Rue Plaetis, L-2338, Luxembourg
VAT number : GB727255821

Please note - this is not a returns address - for returns - please see above for details of our online returns centre

0/DwLw04TxR/-1 of 1-//2ND_LETTER/econ-uk/6549791/0910-19:00/0907-11:36 Pack Type : A2

Contents

Acknowledgements

This book is situated at the intersection of my research and teaching practice, and would not have been possible without the contributions of the many gifted individuals with whom I have collaborated in both domains.

My colleagues at Mälardalen University inspired and supported me for nearly a decade as I applied my research in the classroom. Karin Molander Danielsson was endlessly willing to discuss issues related to source use and to help develop and try out ways of addressing problems in student writing. Thorsten Schröter and Elisabeth Wulff-Sahlén provided daily reference points for the term 'reflective practitioner'. My new colleagues at Linnaeus University (whom I shall not mention individually, for fear of leaving someone out) have been warmly welcoming, and patient while I finished this book.

Avoiding plagiarism is part of learning to write effectively from sources, and that in turn is part of the larger question of language learning, particularly within the university context. Especially warm thanks go to my colleagues on the English Vocabulary Acquisition project, who have explored these broader issues with me. Better collaborators than Aileen Irvine, Hans Malmström, Špela Mežek and Philip Shaw would be difficult to imagine.

Philip Shaw in particular has accompanied me on my journey of discovery about plagiarism, source use and intertextuality virtually since its inception. He has been willing and enthusiastic in his contributions to our projects, gentle but insightful in his critique, and endlessly generous with his time.

All of these people, and others who are too numerous to name, have contributed to my understanding of the phenomena this book treats, and I am grateful to them.

Introduction

Plagiarism is a problem in our universities, and many teachers feel that dealing with it is a heavy and troublesome part of their role. The purpose of this book is to provide university staff with a better understanding of plagiarism and improved skills for dealing with it, so that they can be more effective and feel more confident in doing so.

Plagiarism is a complex phenomenon and an understanding of its complexities is a precondition for being able to respond to it effectively. Chapter 1 thus presents definitions of plagiarism and analyses its constituent components. This chapter introduces key understandings which lay the foundation for the rest of the book.

A key to solving any problem is understanding its causes; outlining the sources of plagiarism is the task of Chapter 2. Chapter 3 examines the ways plagiarism is currently dealt with in universities. This chapter has two objectives: to orient teachers to the sorts of practices in place, and to highlight problematic aspects which make current practices a poor fit for some types of plagiarism.

A recurrent theme in this book is that an ounce of prevention is worth a pound of cure, and that efforts in handling plagiarism should be proactive, rather than reactive, to the greatest extent possible. A key element in helping students avoid plagiarism is helping them learn how to use sources well. Setting forth what students need to know in order to avoid plagiarism, and what staff can do to help them to that understanding, are the topics of Chapters 4 and 5 respectively. The wider role of academic institutions is addressed in Chapter 6.

The final four chapters in the book set plagiarism in a broader context. Chapter 7 deals with second-language writers and international students. What constitutes better and worse use of sources varies to a great extent across academic disciplines, and these differences are the topic of Chapter 8. Chapter 9 discusses the changing nature of the university classroom, and the implications for the source use/plagiarism problem. Chapter 10 then concludes by placing the issues dealt with in the book in the broader higher education perspective.

Two domains related to plagiarism are *not* explored in any detail in this book. One is the intersection of intellectual property and copyright infringement. While plagiarism can overlap with these concepts, in the context of higher education it usually does not. (For a discussion of the ways in which copyright infringement and plagiarism are distinct, see Stearns, 1999.) The other is academic integrity, which is a broad area, but although it subsumes at least some instances of plagiarism, it is clear from the research literature that plagiarism is a more complex question than most other violations of academic ethics, and deserves separate treatment. The review of the causes of plagiarism in Chapter 2 does, however, discuss the research literature on academic dishonesty, and the reader who is interested in pursuing that area further will find the references there a good starting point.

This book, like any volume addressing the continuing professional development needs of university staff, will be used in a variety of settings, but it is assumed that most readers will have a common goal: to learn to handle plagiarism more effectively. The ideas in this book provide a starting point for that objective, but achieving it entails applying these ideas to teaching practice. To this end, this book contains a series of activities which enable readers to deepen their understanding, experience some of the practical challenges of dealing with plagiarism and measure the ideas introduced in the book against the reality of the reader's institutional context.

The starting point for the activities is that reactions to plagiarism differ, in part because institutions vary in their local rules, policies and practices, and in part because individuals also differ in their understandings of, and reactions to, plagiarism. While the chapters in this book describe how plagiarism occurs and how it is, can and should be addressed, the activities link these ideas to the reader's specific institutional context. They ask readers to gather policy documents, analyse student writing and interview staff and students in order to build a portrait of their local situation, and what that implies for dealing with plagiarism and source use issues.

Teachers, writing centre consultants and administrators who are reading this book as a solo enterprise are encouraged to work through the activities, as that will help solidify the ideas presented here. When this book is used as part of a staff development course the activities can form the basis of an assessment task, if one is needed. Although presented chapter by chapter, the activities are connected by a coherent thread and lend themselves to being written up in report form. Because the answers produced in response to each task will vary according to the specifics of the reader's teaching context, no key is provided.

Some readers of this book will be staff developers, and will want to arrive at a better understanding of this phenomenon in order to help colleagues improve their teaching practice. In addition to the activities, each chapter concludes with several questions which can be used for discussion on the learning platform, in a seminar, or as a basis for reflections in a learning log. The book concludes with an appendix giving a plan for a staff-development seminar on plagiarism and source use, and another with case studies which can be used as the starting point for discussion in such a seminar.

Plagiarism is not only a concern for teachers; staff who work in writing centres, study-skills resource rooms, as student advisors, etc., need to tell students about plagiarism and source use, and to do so they need to have a good understanding of the phenomenon. This book is intended to be used by anyone in a student-facing role. When for simplicity's sake I say 'lecturers' and 'teachers', I am writing for that wider group.

Plagiarism is difficult and unpleasant when teachers confront it in the classroom, and may therefore appear an equally unpleasant matter to read about. However, this complex and multi-faceted phenomenon relates to core academic values. These go beyond the simple issue of intellectual property and the right of the author to be acknowledged as such, and touch on more fundamental questions such as how we know which ideas are our own and which other influences deserve to be acknowledged. Improving teaching practice in the area of plagiarism and source use is therefore not only a process of finding a solution to an educational problem; engaging with plagiarism intellectually has an exciting potential to illuminate broad areas of the academic enterprise.

Part One

Understanding plagiarism

1

What is plagiarism?

Summary

Most university lecturers know what plagiarism is but many struggle with unclear cases or the complexities of applying definitions to specific cases of potential plagiarism. University regulations routinely provide definitions and examples of these are taken up and discussed in this chapter. Four criteria for plagiarism are identified. The fourth of these, the intent to deceive, is contentious, and is thus discussed extensively, concluding that policies which exclude intention as a criterion may do so to avoid providing a loophole, rather than out of a conviction that it is irrelevant.

University teachers have been shown to have difficulty deciding if writing is plagiarised, and thus to reach inconsistent determinations about where the threshold for transgression lies. Their process of reasoning often involves the four criteria but subjectivity involved in evaluating work against these criteria places significant pressure on staff and creates a difficult situation for students.

While it is challenging to provide evidence for an increase in the incidence of plagiarism, it is undoubtedly widespread, so action is needed. Focusing efforts on detection and punishment is necessary but insufficient. University students need the skills to use source materials appropriately and properly in their writing.

When you have finished reading this chapter, you will be able to discuss how plagiarism can be defined and characterised, and identify some of the difficulties involved in applying this theoretical understanding to specific cases. You will also have a sense of the scale of the problem, and what that implies for preventing and responding to plagiarism.

Consider what you know and believe about plagiarism in relation to the quotations below. The first two point to different understandings of plagiarism. Which matches your understanding more closely? The third and fourth suggest that plagiarism, while a matter of concern for most teachers, may not be a problem on which many have reflected extensively or have expertise. How closely does that match your experience?

Textual ownership *means* 'These thoughts and phrasings are mine, not yours, and if you use them without attributing them to me, you have committed the worst academic sin of all, plagiarism'.

(Elbow, 1999: 330)

Many novices struggle to figure out exactly how to incorporate others' work into their own, whether in quoting, paraphrasing, summarizing, echoing, or engaging in other forms of conscious and unconscious incorporation.

(Blum, 2010: 26)

Even without being able to articulate a precise definition, many people find it easy to recognize plagiarism – as with pornography, they know it when they see it.

(Stearns, 1999: 7)

In fact, most of us have little knowledge of the 'discipline' of plagiarism – its definitions and theories – even though most of us must teach our students about it. Granted, the concept of plagiarism is not a discipline of its own, but the amount of attention we in the academy are devoting to the issues surrounding it warrants some careful thought beyond who is guilty and what we can do about the perceived problem.

(Day, 2008: 46)

Introduction

The overarching purpose of this chapter is to explore the concept of plagiarism, to survey the definitions and understandings associated with it. This is necessary in part because plagiarism is understood in greatly divergent ways, as the quotations above illustrate. Not only do they frame plagiarism differently – as a sin or a misunderstanding – there is an implication that different processes – committing an inappropriate act, or struggling towards an understanding – underlie the distinction.

To the extent that diverse and even contradictory understandings of plagiarism exist (and it will be seen later in this chapter that this is the case), it may come about in part because plagiarism is a side issue for most teachers; an unfortunate by-product of the main focus of their efforts, which is teaching and assessing student learning in their professional areas.

Thus, while plagiarism is a familiar concept, and most university teachers feel reasonably confident that they know what it is, that certainty can be eroded when less clear-cut cases present themselves, and knowing how to respond to plagiarism requires something more than an instinctive recognition of it. The purpose of this chapter is to examine the way plagiarism is defined in academic settings and the features which characterise it, as well as some of the difficulties involved in recognising it in practice. This will lay a foundation for the discussion of causes and solutions in later chapters.

Defining plagiarism

The following definitions are taken from university policy and regulatory documents, and are broadly typical of the ways universities define and explain plagiarism. (Please note: all errors and other non-standard features in the examples were present in the originals. For sources of examples, see Appendix C.)

Example 1.1

Academic Integrity Statement: Appendix 1

Plagiarism is the reproduction or paraphrasing, without acknowledgement, from **public or private (ie: unpublished)** material (including material downloaded from the internet) attributable to, or which is the intellectual property of, another including the work of students.

Plagiarism may be of written and also non-written form and therefore would also include the unacknowledged use of computer programs, mathematical/computer models/algorithms, computer software in all forms, macros, spreadsheets, web pages, databases, mathematical deviations and calculations, designs/models/displays of any sort, diagrams, graphs, tables, drawings, works of art of any sort, fine art pieces or artefacts, digital images, computer-aided design drawings, GIS files, photographs, maps, music/composition of any sort, posters, presentations and tracing.**

** (this is not an exhaustive list).

Examples of plagiarism are:

- Including in your own work extracts from another person's work without the use of quotation marks and crediting the source.
- The use of the ideas of another person without acknowledgement of the source.
- Paraphrasing or summarising another person's work without acknowledgement.
- Cutting and pasting from electronic sources without explicit acknowledgement of the source of the URL or author and/or without explicitly marking the pasted text as a quotation.
- Submitting a piece of work entirely as your own when it was produced in collaboration with others, and not declaring that this collaboration has taken place (this is known as 'collusion').
- Submitting appropriated imagery or creative products without indicating the source of the work.

As one means of detecting plagiarism, some Schools now use software to check assignments for evidence of plagiarism.

(From a set of university-wide regulations at a British university)

Example 1.2

Plagiarism – the presentation of another's words or ideas as if they were one's own, including but not limited to:

- Submitting, as your own, through purchase or otherwise, part of or an entire work produced verbatim by someone else
- Paraphrasing ideas, data, or writing without properly acknowledging the source
- Unauthorized transfer and use of another person's computer file as your own
- Unauthorized use of another person's data in completing a computer exercise

(From a student guide on academic integrity from a US university; the same definition is found on a resource guide to 'avoiding plagiarism' from the university's library.)

Example 1.3

What is Plagiarism?

Plagiarism is presenting someone else's work as if it were your own, whether you mean to or not.

'Someone else's work' means anything that is not your own idea. Even if it is presented in your own style, you must still acknowledge your sources fully and appropriately. This includes:

- material from books, journals or any other printed source
- the work of other students or staff
- information from the Internet
- software programs and other electronic material
- designs and ideas
- the organisation or structuring of any such material.

Plagiarism undermines academic integrity simply because it is a form of lying, stealing and mistreating others. Plagiarism involves stealing other people's intellectual property and lying about whose work it is. This is why plagiarism is prohibited at [University].

(From an on-line study guide at a New Zealand university)[i]

Although different in level of detail and in some of the specifics that they include, these definitions are in broad agreement with each other. One important point which is illustrated by the more detailed definitions in particular is that plagiarism can involve a wide range of types of materials: ideas and words, but also programming code, images, or indeed an organisational structure. In short, anything which can be said to be original, proprietary, the brainchild of a specific creator, can be plagiarised. As Chapter 8 will discuss, there is a cross-curricular element to this as well; since the sorts of materials used as sources or produced as assessment work vary across academic disciplines, so do the kinds of sources which are likely to be plagiarised. A feature of all plagiarism, though, is that it involves material of some sort which has been appropriated, resulting in a new text. ('Text' is used here in the broadest sense possible, to mean all language, whether written or spoken, as well as non-linguistic material, such as music, photographs, charts, and so on. Because of a practical need to avoid repeatedly referring to the plagiarised product and its sources as 'words, ideas, images, music, etc.', the term 'text' will be used throughout this book, but should be understood in this broader sense.) Simply thinking about taking someone's idea, or words, etc., is not plagiarism; the plagiarism is not complete until the source material is expressed in some way.

The definitions above state or imply four criteria which are fundamental to plagiarism, and which can be used to identify it. First, and somewhat obviously, there must be a relationship of similarity between two texts. The question of whether Agatha Christie's *Murder on the Orient Express* plagiarises Shakespeare's *Hamlet* is not a relevant one; they are fundamentally different works. Although this criterion is very straightforward as a matter of principle (and therefore requires little discussion), the next section will show that it can be difficult to determine in practice when it has been fulfilled.

Second, the similarity exists because the later work (Text B) was based on the earlier one (Text A). This criterion is evidenced in the definitions above in phrases such as 'including in your own work extracts **from** another person's work' (emphasis added). This criterion excludes, for example, the 'infinite monkey theorem', the idea that if a monkey played with a typewriter for an infinite period of time, typing letters at random, eventually the monkey would produce *Hamlet*. If the monkey did so, the result would be a coincidence, not plagiarism.

In addition to coincidence, this criterion excludes the similarities which come about because two texts are on the same topic and/or are exemplars of the same genre. Any two guidebooks to South Africa, selected at random, are likely to have sections on Johannesburg, Cape Town and Kruger Park, and pictures of elephants and giraffes, but those similarities are determined by the topic itself. They are also likely to have introductory sections on the history of the country, and that shared characteristic is dictated by the convention of the genre that says that guide books typically begin with a potted history of the country in question. These likenesses are not in themselves indicative of plagiarism.

A third criterion is that the intertextual relationship is not appropriate. This is seen in language in the definitions such as 'without acknowledgement' and 'you must still acknowledge your sources fully and appropriately'. This criterion excludes properly executed references to other sources, which are of course a standard feature of academic writing. There are many ways, more or less direct, in which earlier texts can appropriately influence newer ones, and many ways in which the influences can be acknowledged.

Examples of direct relationships include the ones which are indicated by citations or references such as those in the examples below. In Example 1.4, the numbers in square brackets correspond to entries in the reference list at the end of the article. In Example 1.5, the endnote indicated by the superscript numeral gives the page reference for the source which is named in the text, and the reference list gives full bibliographical details. Both of these references fulfil the first two criteria for plagiarism in that there is a similarity between the articles from which the examples are taken and their sources, and that relationship exists because an assertion (in the case of 1.4) and words (in the case of 1.5) derive from those sources. However, because this relationship is signalled according to the conventions of the writers' respective disciplines and the requirements of the publications in which they appeared, these are examples of appropriate source use, not plagiarism.

Example 1.4

In-text reference

Considering the diversity of in vitro resistance to antifungal drugs shown by different species of yeasts, their correct identification is a critical aspect of therapeutic planning [7,8].

Reference list entries

7 Kitch TT, Jacobs MR, McGinnis MR, Appelbaum PC. Ability of RapID Yeast Plus System to identify clinically significant yeasts within 5 hours. J Clin Microbiol 1996; 34(5): 1069–1071.
8 Schuffenecker I, Freydiére A, DeMontclos H, Gille Y. Evaluation of four commercial systems for identification of medically important yeasts. Eur J Clin Microbiol Infect Dis 1993; 12(4): 255–260.

Example 1.5

In-text reference

As Haakonssen has argued, Thomasius (1655–1728) 'formulated a theory of natural law as the specification and rule of the passions that make social life possible'.[6]

Endnote

6 Haakonssen, "German Natural Law," 252.

Reference list entry

Haakonssen, Knud. "German natural law." In The Cambridge History of Eighteenth-Century Political Thought, ed. M. Goldie and R. Wokler (Cambridge 2006), 251–90.

The conventional nature of the examples above comes from the fact that the sources they use are acknowledged directly. A range of less explicit relationships are also frequently and appropriately used. One of these is allusion, a reference to a source which is unnamed because the reader is expected to be able to recognise it. Thus the authors of Example 1.6 expected the reader to recognise the opening line of *Pride and Prejudice*: 'It is a truth universally acknowledged, that a single man in possession of a large fortune must be in want of a wife' (Austen, 1813/1995: 3).

Example 1.6

It is a truth universally acknowledged that a medical intervention justified by observational data must be in want of verification through a randomised controlled trial.

In her engaging volume about students and plagiarism, Susan Blum spells out the conventional status of allusion:

[Students] are trying to fulfil so many different purposes, believing many more than six impossible things before breakfast. (That's an allusion to Lewis Carroll's *Through the Looking Glass* – assumed to be common knowledge, and therefore not in need of citation. So my quoting it is not plagiarism, even though I did take it directly from Carroll without crediting my source (2010: 6).

The conventions regarding what sorts of source use are appropriate vary across domains. Journalists, for instance, frequently identify their sources only by name, or indeed allow them to remain anonymous, a situation which is very different from the detailed information which academic writers must usually provide. Further, within the academic community, there are significant differences across subject areas (for example, allusion is much more common in some fields than others), a topic taken up in Chapter 8. Despite differences in the specifics, the basic principle is the same across disciplines and domains: textual re-use which has been rendered appropriate according to the applicable conventions is not plagiarism. Plagiarism requires that material be re-used in an inappropriate way.

The fourth criterion is that plagiarism requires intention. In fact, it requires intention of two sorts. First, the plagiarist must be aware of having copied. A legitimate error in copying and pasting (always assuming that it can be demonstrated that a legitimate error was involved) is not plagiarism. Second, the plagiarist must have intended the copying to be transgressive, i.e., to be a deceptive act. An allusion to a source which is *not* recognised by the reader is a misjudgement, not plagiarism.

The idea that this second sort of intention is criterial in identifying plagiarism is to some extent contentious; in fact, definition three, above, explicitly states the opposite: 'plagiarism is presenting someone else's work as if it were your own, *whether you mean to or not*' (emphasis added). In a survey of university plagiarism policies (Pecorari, 2001), intention was the sole point on which policies were found to be contradictory, with some including language such as that found in the third definition. There are nonetheless a number of reasons for concluding that plagiarism in its central sense involves intentional deception.

One reason is that this appears to be the majority view; in the study cited above, policies stating that intention is irrelevant were in the minority. Other commentary on plagiarism definitions agrees: 'common themes emerge in most expositions of the construct, usually involving the notions of intent, *deliberate* deception and failure to acknowledge sources' (Bennett, 2005: 138).

The sense that the received view of plagiarism involves intention is reinforced by the manner in which teachers react to specific instances of inappropriate source use. In interviews with Australian academics, Bretag found that they 'spent considerable time attempting to distinguish between deliberate and unintentional plagiarism' (2004: 5). In another study, university teachers were shown student writing and asked to say whether it was plagiarised, and their process of decision-making usually took intention into account. When some other reasonable explanation for unacceptable source use presented itself, for example, if they thought that the student was unfamiliar with what the rules required, they disassociated themselves from the label 'plagiarism' (Pecorari and Shaw, 2012).

This conclusion is also supported by the wording in definitions. All but the first of those above use the phrase 'as if it were your own', or some close variation on it (e.g., 'as one's own). Using something 'as one's own' (when, by clear implication, it is not actually one's own) is necessarily an act of pretence. Other words which frequently arise in policies are 'making use of', 'presenting', and 'passing off', and all of these actions involve a degree of conscious awareness. 'Passing off' is a common euphemism for fraud or deception. This is acknowledged implicitly by Example 1.3. After declaring that intention is not relevant, it goes on to say that 'Plagiarism undermines academic integrity simply because it is a form of lying, stealing and mistreating others'. Lying, however, is stating what one knows or believes to be untrue. If plagiarism is a form of lying, then it must also be a sort of deception. Stealing is also an intentional act. Thus, even definitions which assert explicitly that intentional deceit is not criterial in identifying plagiarism nonetheless appear tacitly to accept that it really is.

If this is the case, it is both reasonable and consistent with the frequent metaphorical treatment of plagiarism as a crime. Policies use the rhetoric of crime and punishment, and official procedures for handling the act are often quasi-judicial in nature, with disciplinary boards listening to, and weighing up, the evidence from the 'accuser' and the 'accused'. A fundamental precept in English common law, adopted by those countries whose legal codes are based on common law (e.g., Australia, the US), and also found in other countries, is that *mens rea*, the state of mind of an offender, must be taken into account in most criminal offences, and the absence of an intention to commit the crime in question means that no crime occurred. If a student takes a classmate's copy of their textbook by mistake, because two copies of the same book are easily confused, the taking is not an act of theft because the student did not intend to deprive the classmate of his or her property.

What, then is the basis for the stipulations found in some policies that intention is not relevant? Discussing the process of revising a university plagiarism policy, Devlin reports that it was decided 'to remove the phrase "with intent to deceive", which was seen by both staff and students as a loophole' (2006: 4) and it seems likely that that reasoning may be widespread. If plagiarism policies proclaimed that the same use of text from a source was either an act of academic misconduct or an honest mistake, then every student accused of plagiarism would claim the latter explanation. The stipulation that plagiarism can happen unintentionally may not be motivated so much by a belief that an honest mistake should be treated as plagiarism, as by a desire to prevent the guilty from avoiding punishment by claiming that they did not mean to offend. Intention, after all, is extremely difficult to establish, and it is as difficult to prove that an offender did *not* mean to do wrong as it is for the offender to prove the opposite. In saying 'whether you mean to or not', policy makers may actually mean '(claimed) ignorance of the law is no excuse'.

Thus, while acknowledging that there are a variety of views on the topic, and some individuals may view intention as irrelevant, there are good reasons to believe that the common understanding of plagiarism in its prototypical sense involves wilful deception. Throughout this book, the need will arise from time to time to distinguish between these two senses of plagiarism. The term *prototypical plagiarism* will be used to refer to textual re-use which meets all four of the criteria above, including an intention on the part of the writer to repeat the earlier text, and an intention to deceive the reader thereby.

To indicate source use which meets the first three criteria but not the fourth, the term *patchwriting* will be used. This term was coined by Rebecca Moore Howard (1995) to describe the strategies of inexperienced writers who feel they need support in order to produce academic writing, and lean too heavily on their sources for that support. In Howard's usage, patchwriting has a number of specific causes (which are discussed in Chapter 2). Here the term will be extended slightly and used for any sort of unintentional plagiarism. The importance of this distinction will be seen especially in Chapters 4 and 5, which deal with learning and teaching as a means of preventing plagiarism, as prevention requires an understanding of the source of the problem.

However, it is not always possible to understand what a writer's intentions were, and in some cases intention is not directly relevant in deciding the best way to respond to inappropriate source use. Where it is not necessary to distinguish between prototypical plagiarism and patchwriting, the term *textual plagiarism* will be used, to indicate writing which meets the first three of the criteria outlined above – those which can be established on the basis of textual features, without reference to the writer's intention. Textual plagiarism disregards the issue of intention, and is used as umbrella term, with both patchwriting and prototypical plagiarism as subtypes. Where the word *plagiarism*, unqualified, is used, it refers to this broader concept as well. Table 1.1 shows the characteristics associated with these three terms.

Table 1.1 Working definitions of plagiarism

	Textual plagiarism	Prototypical plagiarism	Patchwriting
Text A and Text B are similar.	yes	yes	yes
The similarity is caused by Text B being based on Text A.	yes	yes	yes
The re-use of Text A is appropriate.	no	no	no
The writer of Text B • intends to re-use Text A, • and in doing so intends to deceive.	not known	yes	no

Problems in applying the criteria

The criteria identified above, taken together, cover the characteristics which the act of plagiarism is commonly understood to have, and with the possible exception of intention, there is broad agreement on them. However, if defining plagiarism is fairly straightforward, applying definitions of it to specific cases is not. University teachers have been shown to behave inconsistently in determining when a text constitutes plagiarism (Roig, 2001). When attempting to reach a decision, they frequently explain their difficulty in deciding with reference to the four criteria. Specifically, it may not be clear whether one or more of them is present (Pecorari and Shaw, 2012). Because a suspicion of plagiarism must be resolved, whether by a teacher who wonders whether it should be taken to another level, or by a disciplinary panel that must decide on a case, this uncertainty is problematic, so it is worth reviewing some of the aspects which present difficulty.

Examples 1.7, 1.8 and 1.9 feature an extract from a piece of student writing (above in each example) and the student's source (the second in each pair). Before reading further, look at each pair and consider whether in your view it exemplifies acceptable source use or not. If unacceptable, does it constitute plagiarism or not?

Example 1.7

Student

The genus *Mentha* (Laminaceae) is composed of 19 geographically widespread species and 13 named natural. Peppermint (*Mentha* × piperita) and spearmint are grown world-wide as perennial herbs, and produce different essential oils which are used as flavourings.

Source

Mentha is a genus of wide distribution and considerable economic importance. Shoots and leaves of several species are often used as a condiment. The essential oils, which are steam distilled from the herbage, are processed into flavourings for food, medicine, mouthwash, toothpaste and powder, chewing gum, and candy. In modern taxonomic treatments of the genus (Harley and Brighton, 1977), there are five sections (*Mentha* sect. *Audibertia*, sect. *Eriodontes*, sect. *Mentha*, sect. *Preslia*, and sect. *Pulegium*) containing 19 species and 13 named hybrids involving species of *M.* sect *Mentha*.

Example 1.8

Student

Reed (1999) reported that 50% of the mint cultures in National Clonal Germplasm Repository (NCGR) under slow growth conditions were lost due to the fungal or bacterial contamination.

Source

Some clonal crops are kept in slow-growth storage as in vitro cultures for germplasm conservation (Ashmore, 1997; Engelmann, 1991; Withers, 1991; Withers *et al.*, 1990). Previously, mint cultures held at the National Clonal Germplasm Repository (NCGR) were stored at 4 °C in darkness in 13×100 mm glass tubes on MS (Murashige and Skoog, 1962) medium. Under these storage conditions, 50% of the cultures were lost to fungal or bacterial contamination (Reed, unpublished data).

Example 1.9

Student

Brassica oleracea is an important vegetable crop species, which includes fully cross-fertile cultivars or form groups with widely different morphological characteristics, such as cabbage, broccoli, cauliflower, Brussels sprout and kohlrabi. Genetic studies has been limited because long generation time of the biennials, the complex inheritance patterns of some trait, and the difficulty in overcoming self-incompatibility.

> **Source**
> *Brassica oleracea* is an important vegetable crop species which includes fully cross-fertile cultivars or form groups with widely-differing morphological characteristics (cabbage, broccoli, cauliflower, collards, Brussels sprouts, kohlrabi, and kale). Genetic studies of *B. oleracea* have been limited in part by the long generation time of the biennials, the complex inheritance patterns of some traits, and the difficulty in overcoming self-incompatibility.

Establishing similarity between two texts

The pairs of extracts in each example above have a topic in common, and as a result also have some shared wording. However, this is the relationship which will always exist between any source and the text which cites it. Citations serve to support an idea which has been articulated in the new text. If there were no point of contact between the two, a citation to the source would be irrelevant. The question here then becomes 'How similar is similar?' This leads naturally to examining the next criterion; is it similar enough to suggest a causal relationship?

Establishing a relationship between two texts

An element which teachers draw on when trying to decide whether the similarities between two texts came about because one was based on the other is often quantity: how much of the source is repeated in the new text; and what proportion of the new text is made up of material from the putative source? There is a sense that, all other things being equal, the greater the similarity of content or language, the greater the likelihood that the newer text was based upon the earlier one. Describing the degree of similarity is not difficult. (Indeed, a quantitative measure of similarity is what text-matching software, sometimes called 'plagiarism detection' tools, rely on. This topic is taken up in Chapter 3.) From a purely quantitative perspective we can say that Example 1.7 consists of 37 words, of which 16, or 43%, also appear in the source. In Example 1.8 there are 28 words, and 21 of these, or 75%, are in the source. Example 1.9 is longer, with 55 words, of which 50, or 91% can be found in the source. However, while it may be the case that more people would be willing to believe that the similarities in 1.7 are coincidental, and fewer would believe that the similarities in 1.9 are coincidental, there is likely to be disagreement. This is because there is no established 'threshold level' which can be taken to be indicative of copying, rather than coincidence (the absence of a 'threshold level' constitutes a limitation on the usefulness of 'plagiarism detection' software; this will be addressed in Chapter 3).

In addition, all other things are rarely equal. That is to say, some language is more likely to be repeated coincidentally than other. This contradicts to some extent the idea that most language use is original and creative. The linguist

Steven Pinker calls this idea 'the sheer vastness of language' and proposes this experiment to demonstrate it: 'go into the Library of Congress and pick a sentence at random from any volume, and chances are you would fail to find an exact repetition no matter how long you continued to search' (1994: 85). However, much of the language we produce is formulaic in nature, so while that statement may be true for any given sentence found at random, it is not at all difficult to identify sentences which may be found in multiple places.

Our daily language is full of expressions like 'I'm sorry, would you mind . . .' and 'If you'll just excuse me . . .' and 'Would it be possible to . . .?' Academic language is similarly full of formulaic units such as 'it remains to be seen whether' or 'an important distinction to make is between'. Consider a sentence like this: 'The strains used are shown in Table 1'. Searching for that exact string on Google Scholar produces 86 hits (or did in mid-2012). If the table number is not specified, the number of hits rises to 122. Yet there is no reason to believe that the authors of these 122 research articles copied the phrase from each other, or from some common source; identifying the strains of an organism used in research is a common function in a research article in biology, listing them in a table is also common, and therefore a reference to the table is to all intents and purposes mandatory. There are other expressions which would accomplish the same task (for example, 'the strains used in *this experiment*' or 'in *these experiments*' can also be found) but the phrase is such a standard one that it is bound to recur again and again.

Standard, formulaic expressions may be thought to be less indicative of copying than unusual, creative, less frequent wordings, and by the same token facts which are less well known than others. The fact that the essential oils derived from mint are used as flavouring is not a closely guarded secret; however, the ideas found in Example 1.4 about drug resistance in some species of yeast are probably less widely known, and their co-occurrence in two texts may be considered a stronger indication of a direct relationship. However, once again, while the status of words and ideas as more or less common may be a factor in deciding whether Text B was based on Text A, there is no litmus test to indicate where texts should be placed on that continuum.

Other factors could be added to this list; for example, 1.9 not only shares more words with its source, it contains longer strings of words found in the source in the same order than 1.7 or 1.8. However, any observations about the degree of similarity between two texts runs up against the same wall: there is no formula for working out what sort of similarity can coincidentally occur. The uncertainty arises because this criterion – that Text B was based on Text A – is related to the writing process, but evidence for or against that direct, causal relationship is, like the factors discussed in this section, about the product. Any attempt to look at the written product and try to infer what process produced it will be necessarily impressionistic. This can be a source of discomfort for teachers and others (for example, members of disciplinary boards) who are in the position of having to draw inferences about a process indirectly from the product in order to decide whether student writing is plagiarised. They may reach their conclusions only tentatively, and feel less than fully confident about them.

Establishing an inappropriate relationship

It is a widely accepted academic principle that sources should be acknowledged, that intellectual debts should be recognised. However, beyond this broad principle, the specifics of what constitutes an appropriate, and appropriately signalled, relationship between two texts is subject to debate, and between the fully acceptable and the manifestly wrong there is the less than ideal, which may be acceptable or not.

To some extent this is because variation exists across academic contexts as to what or how sources can or should be used. There is also considerable variation in the conventions about how to signal the appropriate relationships to the reader. Academic disciplines differ greatly from each other in these respects, and Chapter 8 examines that variation in detail.

However, even within the same academic community, different individuals hold greatly differing views as to what is and is not acceptable. When a number of established academics were asked to comment on five examples of source use, including Examples 1.7 and 1.8 above, they disagreed about which ones were appropriate (Pecorari and Shaw, 2012). Several judged 1.7 as acceptable without hesitation or elaboration, but one thought that a reference was needed both because some information and some words derived directly from the source. Another respondent was unable to say whether 1.7 was appropriate or not. The response to 1.8 was similar, though the academic who called it clearly inappropriate was not the same person who thought 1.7 was.

The disagreement about these and other examples was not because there were individual outliers who took a much stricter or much looser view of what is acceptable. The source of their disagreement was that they looked to different factors to help them make their decisions. For example, one looked at the presence or absence of a citation to a source author, while another considered the length of chunks repeated from the source to be an important criterion, and another still tried to weigh up whether the ideas and words which were repeated from the source were commonplace or unique and particular. In other words, they reached different conclusions about the acceptability of a particular way of using a source because they looked to different features in making their judgements.

Disagreement was also the result of a large-scale survey of university teachers in the US who were asked to pass judgement on six paragraphs. Four of the paragraphs had been designed by the researcher to reflect varying degrees of plagiarism while two were intended to exemplify plagiarism-free writing. No paragraph received a unanimous response, and the two paragraphs which were intended to be seen as appropriate were in fact judged to be plagiarism by a small number of respondents (Roig, 2001). In another survey, when academics in a range of roles as well as students were asked to decide whether four paragraphs were plagiarised, there was disagreement both across and within the groups (Julliard, 1994).

Not only do academics disagree with each other, they also find it difficult to decide. In Roig's investigation, up to nine per cent of participants (varying according to the paragraph in question) said they couldn't determine whether plagiarism had occurred. In our study, five of the eight teachers interviewed found it impossible to say whether or not an example was acceptable, in at least one case. Once they had concluded that an example was not acceptable, deciding whether it was plagiarism was harder still.

Establishing intention

Intention is the most difficult of the criteria to establish, in part because it, like the question of whether a source-based writing process was used, cannot be got at directly. Only the writer actually knows whether he or she intended to transgress, and there is a tendency to discount the writer's account, at least if deceptive intention is denied. 'I didn't mean to' is very easy to say, and very difficult to prove or disprove.

In fact, the problem is even more complex because there are two distinct sorts of deliberate behaviour related to plagiarism. The first is whether the re-use of language from a source was intentional. One means by which unintentional plagiarism can arise is through a phenomenon which has been described in the psychology research literature as cryptomnesia (e.g. Brown and Murphy, 1989). Cryptomnesia occurs when a writer reads a source, forgets having done so, and at a later date produces parts of the source in the mistaken belief that it is his or her new and original creation. Writers may also copy and paste from a source into their notes and then later mistakenly believe that they had paraphrased, summarised or otherwise significantly altered the wording of the source. If they then copy directly from their notes into their final text, the final text may contain verbatim wording from the source, but the writer may be unaware of it. In cases like these, the writer may lack the most basic sort of intention, the intention to re-use material from a source.

Beyond that, a writer may be aware of having copied or otherwise re-used material from a source, but may not intend it to transgress rules, or to be deceptive about the textual re-use. In other words, copying may not be perceived as a cheating behaviour. Anecdotal accounts exist of students copying from their lecture notes or the textbook and believing that no citation is necessary because the lecturer would recognise the source, so a citation would be superfluous. Another often heard (and often contested) idea is that students from some cultures view copying from a source as a laudable study skill. Chapters 2 and 7 address the factors leading to unintentional plagiarism more fully.

Teachers trying to understand what a student's intentions were often try to infer them from the textual evidence available. An experienced university teacher commented 'I don't think I've ever discovered *intentional* plagiarism. Do you know what I mean, someone really taking . . . a whole essay, I've never seen that'. For this teacher, length – 'a whole essay' – would have been an indication that the copying was not accidental. For other teachers, factors such as whether the source is named somewhere in the student text, or how common or unique the language is, may be weighed up as evidence for or against deceptive intent. The point, once again, is that they cannot really know what the writer's intention was, and are forced to come to a determination based on circumstantial evidence.

The act Howard (1995) described as *patchwriting* involves more or less elaborate changes to the source: various sources may be combined, with superficial changes such as substituting synonyms for key words, making active verbs passive and vice versa, or adding to, subtracting from or re-ordering the items in a list. Some teachers view the considerable effort these changes take as evidence that the student was not trying to shirk the time-consuming task of writing: if they were looking for an easy way out, they would have copied a whole text, and skipped the process of changing it. Others, though, see making changes as analogous to filing the serial number off stolen property, as evidence of writers attempting to cover their traces, thus suggesting that they have something illicit to hide.

Teachers frequently take into account their impressions of a student's character. One university lecturer in nursing recounted the experience of finding extensive textual plagiarism in the work of a student who was just about to finish her degree. The lecturer concluded that it was an honest mistake and implied that this was because the writer was 'a good student and very ambitious'. The lecturer talked to the student and concluded 'I can't take this further, because really you should take [something like this] further' as a matter for the disciplinary board. Under the procedures in place at that university, taking the matter further would likely have resulted in the student being suspended and concomitant delays, potentially long ones, in completing her degree. Because the lecturer concluded that intentional deception was not involved, she was correct not to report the matter to the disciplinary board, according to the rules in place at that university. However, the difference in outcomes for the student was considerable, and, significantly, the outcome was entirely dependent on the teacher's individual and unsupported assessment of the highly subjective evidence for and against intentional deception. The importance of intention and the subjectivity involved in evaluating it place a heavy burden on staff and create an unstable situation for students.

The incidence of plagiarism

From the preceding discussion it is clear that identifying plagiarism is a problematic, contentious and sometimes haphazard affair, so it is not surprising that pinning down the frequency of plagiarism is very difficult, and figures and estimates diverge considerably. What is clear, though, is that plagiarism is not rare. In a UK study of students' self-reported behaviour, a majority of students were found to have engaged in acts which were equated with plagiarism, although various sorts of textual re-use were reported at different frequencies. Only 20% said they had never copied 'a couple of sentences' while 75% said they had never turned in an entirely plagiarised work (Bennett, 2005: 150). A study of university students in South Africa found plagiarism in a quarter of the 151 essays checked (Ellery, 2008b). Studies which analysed student source use in detail among students writing in their first language (Howard, Serviss and Rodrigue, 2010) or a second language (Pecorari, 2003) have found that all or nearly all repeated language from source texts, with or without minor changes to the wording, produced results which many teachers may describe as plagiarism. A survey of lecturers found that 72% had found plagiarism among their students' work within the last year, and those reported on average approximately three cases per person (Pickard, 2006).

A frequently heard idea is that plagiarism is not only a persistent problem, it is becoming more frequent. It is easier to find this idea asserted than it is to find it supported with evidence. Among the limited data is a 2003 survey of 31 universities carried out by the BBC Radio 4 'World at One' news programme. According to the report, 'nearly eight out of 10 said more students were passing others' work off as their own. A third said they were having to deal with many more such cases compared with a few years ago' ('High Costs'). Another survey of UK universities got responses from nine institutions, and 'only one suggested that there had been no increase in the incidence of plagiarism since the mid-1990s' (Larkham and Manns, 2002: 342). Internationally comparisons are difficult because statistics are not always gathered, and when they are, are not fully comparable. However, in Sweden, where statistics of university disciplinary cases are kept nationwide, they show that the number of reported cases of plagiarism rose from 68 in 2001 to 406 in 2010 (Högskoleverket, 2011: 13).

Apart from the limited number of studies, there are several factors which make it difficult to reach any conclusion about either frequency or trends. One is the difficulty of getting information from the relevant sources. The Larkham and Manns study cited above attempted to survey a sizeable and representative group of universities but many 'simply refused to respond to some or all of the questions on the grounds that such disciplinary actions were confidential' (2002: 342). The methods used for gathering data vary, and include surveys of students' self-reported behaviour and staff reports of the frequency with which they encounter plagiarism, as well as automated and manual analyses of student writing, thus leading to results which are not fully comparable. Operational definitions of plagiarism also differ across studies, and the accuracy of self-reporting depends in part on a shared understanding of plagiarism which – as noted above – is lacking.

A way around this obstacle used in some studies is to ask not about plagiarism, but about the specific acts that are grouped under that label. One, for example, asked students whether they had included 'a couple of' or 'several' sentences in their work without acknowledgement (Bennett, 2005: 148). However, this approach requires students to apply an abstract description to their writing practices, leaving room for misunderstanding or inconsistency. For example students who have included sentences from a source in their assignments but have replaced some words with synonyms may have difficulty knowing whether they should answer 'yes' or 'no'.

Text-based studies comparing student writing to their sources avoid this difficulty but face another, the impossibility of knowing whether all the sources have been found. In addition, for findings to be meaningful, observed similarities between student texts and their sources must be described in terms which allow them to be compared with each other and with working definitions of plagiarism, and this re-introduces the difficulty that different types of source use are viewed very differently by different individuals. In other words, whatever labels or categories are used to describe findings (e.g., '40% repetition from source' or 'no citation present') will subsume information which some individuals would feel they need to see in order to decide whether that degree of repetition, or the absence of a citation, is acceptable or not.

Using statistics of *reported* cases as an index of frequency has the significant limitation that there is no way to know what proportion of cases are found and reported. Deceptive plagiarists try to hide what they've done, and patchwriting is not always detected either. Some teachers who detect plagiarism opt to resolve it outside their university's formal procedures. The number of cases reported represents, therefore, only a proportion of the total incidence of plagiarism. There is, however, no reason to believe that the proportion reported is stable, so that the total can be extrapolated from it. Indeed, it seems likely that the more attention plagiarism receives, the more likely staff are to be aware of it, to be proactive in detecting it, and to be vigilant in reporting it, so a rise in the number of reported cases could both reflect and cause changes in staff behaviour, rather than indicating an increase in student plagiarism.

In all this uncertainty about the prevalence of plagiarism, there are two clear implications for how we deal with it. First, we do know that it is not an isolated phenomenon. If plagiarism were a rare event, there might be a case to be made for treating it entirely or primarily with *post facto* measures, focusing efforts on detection and punishment. Given that it is in fact widespread, addressing plagiarism must involve significant efforts to be proactive.

In addition, as Blum notes, the sheer frequency with which it occurs indicates not 'moral turpitude on a vast scale but . . . evidence that plagiarism is a fundamental and correctable stage of learning how to write' (2010: 27). In other words, efforts to combat it cannot be purely punitive: plagiarism demands a pedagogical response.

The uncertainty around plagiarism and its identification creates a situation which places students in a perilous position, and staff in an uncomfortable struggle with subjectivity, and as a result threatens consistency in assessment and therefore quality in higher education. The focus of the remainder of this book is on equipping staff with the knowledge and skills necessary to cope with this situation and improve outcomes for students.

Activity

An analysis of institutional definitions of plagiarism. Find a definition of plagiarism in use at your university, and analyse it from the perspectives taken up in this chapter. Here are some things to think about.

- Where was the definition: in a discipline policy, in a study guide, etc.?
- How much time did you spend looking for the definition?
- How likely is it that students will find and read it?
- Did you find one definition or several? If the latter, were they mutually consistent?
- In what respects is the definition similar or dissimilar to those presented in this chapter?
- To what extent and in what way does the definition address the four criteria for plagiarism, either directly or by implication?
- If you have encountered something you thought might be plagiarism at first hand, imagine applying the definition you found to that case. To what extent would the definition be helpful to you in deciding whether plagiarism was involved, or convincing someone else that it was (or was not) plagiarism?

Questions for reflection or discussion

1 Some of the factors which can contribute to an understanding of whether plagiarism has occurred were discussed above. Are there other factors which can help make that determination? For example, is the level of the student relevant?

2 How do the figures for the frequency of plagiarism (above) compare with your experience? How frequently have you identified plagiarism in student work? Does your experience suggest that some types of plagiarism are more common than others?

3 If you discuss plagiarism in your teaching (for example, at the beginning of a course), what questions do students have about it? If you have had a conversation with a student about suspected or detected plagiarism, what explanations for it were offered? To what extent does your understanding of plagiarism match the ideas and beliefs students typically have?

2

Why does plagiarism happen?

Summary

This chapter discusses the causes of textual plagiarism in both its forms: prototypical (deceptive) plagiarism, and patchwriting. The role of electronic media and the Internet and the key aspects of study and academic writing skills which contribute to plagiarism are discussed as causes. Not understanding principles for good source use is shown to be an issue, as is a lack of the skills needed to put those principles into practice. While lecturers may have evidence of plagiarism, establishing the reasons for it with certainty is challenging. Nevertheless, an understanding of the possible causes is useful in developing preventive measures; it can also help the teacher and regulator to avoid assumptions about the motivations of the writer, and thus take a balanced view of the situation, increasing the chances of a constructive response to plagiarism when it occurs.

After reading this chapter you will have an understanding of the wide range of factors which can contribute to plagiarism, as well as the complex ways in which they interact. This will serve as a foundation both for evaluating the solutions proposed in the second section of this book, and for helping guide and shape your understanding of and response to plagiarism when you encounter it in your teaching practice.

The two quotations below describe two different forms of plagiarism. The first is Rebecca Moore Howard's description of what she found in her students' writing. The second is from an account by a ghostwriter who published his experiences under a pseudonym. Have you knowingly encountered either of these forms of plagiarism? How common do you believe they are at your institution?

In 1986, one third of the students in my General Education class at a prestigious liberal arts college plagiarized an assigned paper. The sort of plagiarism they committed is what I have come to call 'patchwriting': copying from a source text and then deleting some words, altering grammatical structures, or plugging in one synonym for another. The practice is uniformly banned in composition handbooks and in colleges' academic codes. Even when patchwriting is accompanied by citation and documentation, our standard academic rules label it a transgression subject to punishment.

(Howard, 1999: xvii)

In the past year, I've written roughly 5,000 pages of scholarly literature, most on very tight deadlines. But you won't find my name on a single paper. . . . I've written for courses in history, cinema, labor relations, pharmacology, theology, sports management, maritime security, airline services, sustainability, municipal budgeting, marketing, philosophy, ethics, Eastern religion, postmodern architecture, anthropology, literature, and public administration. I've attended three dozen online universities. I've completed 12 graduate theses of 50 pages or more. All for someone else. You've never heard of me, but there's a good chance that you've read some of my work. I'm a hired gun, a doctor of everything, an academic mercenary. My customers are your students. I promise you that. Somebody in your classroom uses a service that you can't detect, that you can't defend against, that you may not even know exists.

(Dante, 2010)

The previous chapter distinguished between two forms of plagiarism: prototypical plagiarism is a form of cheating, an act of deception in an attempt to gain unearned credit; patchwriting is a merging of sources which is not intentionally deceptive but is indicative of a developmental stage in learning the skills and techniques of academic writing. This distinction suggests that the causes of plagiarism are likely to resolve into two separate questions: why do students cheat? and what causes patchwriting? This chapter begins by addressing the first, with a review of the causes of academic dishonesty.

However, in practice the causes of these two types of plagiarism often blur together, in part because the distinction between dishonest and appropriate behaviour is not always clear for students: they perceive grey areas in which they are unsure of the expectations placed upon them; or they perceive ethical behaviour differently than staff do (Ashworth, Bannister and Thorne, 1997). Thus a writing strategy which a teacher sees as over-reliance on the language of a source (for example) may be caused either by a belief on the part of the student that the strategy is appropriate, or by a need to cut corners. The second half of this chapter thus conflates these two types of plagiarism and discusses the causes of strategies which exist in the shadowlands of academic writing practice. One issue – the role of culture/second-language status – falls under this category but will be discussed in Chapter 7.

Why do students cheat (by plagiarising)?

The research literature on academic ethics has demonstrated a variety of reasons why students engage in dishonest behaviour in general, and in plagiarism as a form of cheating in particular. A broad distinction can be made between two sorts of explanations: the reasons which impel students to cheat, and the reasons they feel can justify or excuse cheating behaviour.

The risk of negative consequences is a factor militating against cheating. Warnings that cheating will be punished (Davis and Ludvigson, 1995) and a belief that they are likely to be detected (Selwyn, 2008) makes students report that they are less likely to cheat. The perception that staff do not detect it was offered by students as a cause of plagiarism in LoCastro and Masuko's (2002) study.

The penalties attendant upon detection have also been identified as a factor. 'I knew if I got caught nothing would happen' was given as a reason for cheating in one study (Davis, Grover, Becker and McGregor, 1992: 17), and Bennett (2005) found that concern about penalties caused students not to plagiarise. However, McCabe and Trevino (1997) found the opposite relationship in their large-scale survey: severe penalties correlated with more cheating behaviour, not less. They suggest, though, that this may be because students who have cheated have paid closer attention to the penalties than those who have not, and indeed have possibly suffered them.

Having insufficient time has been identified as a cause of plagiarism (Locastro and Masuko, 2002) and cheating more generally (Franklyn-Stokes and Newstead, 1995), and this may be particularly true if students are working at paid jobs in addition to their studies (Bennett, 2005). Time management issues take other forms as well. The balance between the difficulty of course content and the time allotted to it may leave students stretched. This can lead them to form study groups which unintentionally edge over the boundary into collusion, or to them feeling sufficient pressure to make deliberate cheating seem justifiable.

Grades also exert a pressure; to attain a better grade is one reason students give for cheating (Franklyn-Stokes and Newstead, 1995) and having poor grades was found to correlate with a greater likelihood of plagiarising (Bennett, 2005). This is, naturally, a factor which interacts with others: an ambitious student who has his or her sights set on top marks but feels a course expects too much in too little time may perceive unattractive alternatives: to cheat or to shed ambitions.

Some students feel less a part of the university, and more hesitant to subscribe to its values, than others. Another finding from Bennett's study (2005) was that the absence of 'academic integration' correlated with a greater likelihood of plagiarising. Alienation may be one effect of the commercialisation of higher education, the idea that 'the discourse of "consumer" has partially replaced the discourse of "student"' (Ashworth, Freewood and Macdonald, 2003: 258), and that in turn may lead some students to feel less of a vested interest in complying with academic rules and upholding standards.

The role of peers appears to be a mixed and complex one. McCabe and Trevino (1997) found that peer disapproval made it less likely that students would cheat, and that they were more likely to cheat if they thought their peers did, or if they were members of a fraternity or sorority (and a reasonable assumption is that the latter category entails the former). The students in Sutton and Taylor's (2011) survey reported that they felt under pressure to share their work with friends, and other studies have found that friendship was seen as a good reason for letting a friend cheat (Davis *et al.*, 1992; Franklyn-Stokes and Newstead, 1995).

Blum explains this in terms of the value university students have been taught to place on social relationships:

> Students have been raised to be sociable, and they like to work together, to be in groups. One of the greatest forms of praise, which I heard over and over, is that someone is 'really outgoing'. When young people spend time together living, studying, preparing, eating, partying, they are less concerned about tracing influences from one person to another. After all, haven't we told them since early childhood that one of the primary virtues is sharing?
>
> (2010: 5)

Interestingly, though, while agreeing that 'to help a friend' was a reason to cheat, in the Franklyn-Stokes and Newstead study (1995), 'peer pressure' was not. This suggests that students see a distinction between an independent decision to help a friend, which is legitimate, and being pressured into doing so, which is not.

That implies that student views of cheating and appropriate behaviour are not always aligned with those of staff, and indeed that is the case. One aspect of this situation is that students report being unclear about what sort of behaviours are acceptable (Locastro and Masuko, 2002; Sutton and Taylor, 2011; Yeo, 2007). Another is that students have different perceptions from staff. Norton, Tilley, Newstead and Franklyn-Stokes (2001) found a positive correlation between students' self-reported behaviour with regard to acts which are legitimate behaviours but were strategic efforts to get a high mark, such as using polysyllabic words to impress the lecturer, and some cheating behaviours. It is possible that students see these acts as being on a continuum rather than belonging to two discrete categories, honest and dishonest.

This resonates with Ashworth, Bannister and Thorne's (1997) finding that students saw cheating and plagiarism as moral issues, but put their own interpretation on the morality, with the result that they believed that 'some punishable behaviour can be regarded as justifiable and some officially approved behaviour can be felt to be dubious' (187). Thus, while cheating is real and is the cause of some plagiarism, much behaviour which staff wish to discourage is seen by students as something other than a deliberate flouting of the rules.

Shades of intention

Despite the fact that academics hold diverse views about which acts constitute plagiarism, a stable perception in academia is that plagiarism (however we conceive of it) is an act of serious wrongdoing, and one which is frequently condemned in strong language: 'plagiarism is widely thought of as perhaps the most grievous academic crime' (Rosamond, 2002: 167); Kolich quotes a colleague 'in a rage of indignation' as declaring 'nothing is so vile or obscene as the insult of plagiarism. It's the worm of reason!' (1983: 144). This applies to researchers as well as teachers: 'this crime refers to stealing someone else's work or ideas, and passing it off as one's own. For a researcher, this form of scientific misconduct represents fraud of the worst order' (Peh and Arokiasamy, 2008: 965); 'incidents of plagiarism . . . corrupt the souls of the perpetrators' (Betts, 1992: 289).

However, for students those perceptions may not be equally categorical, or equally strong. Students have unclear ideas about what they are and are not allowed to do with their sources. One implication of this is that those who know that there is an act called plagiarism which they are supposed to avoid may not understand how seriously it is viewed by their teachers and other gatekeepers. Relative newcomers to the academic community may produce textual plagiarism, and may even do so intentionally, but the intention may not be as extreme as to commit a soul-corrupting act. If plagiarism can be equated with a crime, as the quotations above suggest, it should be remembered that not all crimes are equally serious, nor the circumstances equally aggravated.

What a teacher sees as the scholarly equivalent of murder, deserving 'the academic death penalty' (Howard, 1995) may be perceived by the student as being on a par with crossing against a red light: technically wrong, but not so very wrong.

Thus it is clear that the boundary between unintentional and deliberate plagiarism is not always sharply demarcated. The sections which follow describe causes which can explain plagiarism of both sorts.

Electronic media

The idea that the Internet and other forms of electronic communication cause plagiarism is one reason offered for the often-asserted claim that there has been a dramatic increase in the incidence of plagiarism. Like that claim, it is easier to find articulations of this idea than evidence to support it. As Ellery notes, while 'a number of authors contend that this ease of access to information from electronic sources has contributed to the increase in student plagiarism at tertiary institutions in recent years. . . . . no empirical studies in this regard have been located' (2008a: 607). In fact, one study of Internet plagiarism found students reporting approximately balanced use of the Internet and print sources for textual plagiarism (Selwyn, 2008; it must be noted that things change quickly on the Internet, and patterns of usage may have altered since that study was conducted).

The rise of Internet-based paper mills, sites where students can either order bespoke assignments written to the terms of their assignment, or download essays 'off the rack', has garnered a great deal of attention. In 2010, when the *Chronicle of Higher Education* published the account of a writer who earns a living producing assignments for students who cannot, or choose not, to write their own assessment work (quoted above), it provoked outraged reactions. However similar practices – handing in a 'recycled' paper written by a friend or older sister who took the course earlier, or commissioning a custom-written assignment from a bright fellow-student – predate the Internet and currently co-exist with electronically mediated plagiarism.

A reason frequently offered for the supposed popularity of the Internet as a source for less wholesale plagiarism is the sheer ease of it: the mechanics of copying and pasting are less labour-intensive in the computer age, and the wealth of material out there to be copied from is vast, and available at the click of a mouse, saving would-be plagiarists the effort of a trip to the library. While both these things are true, they only help explain those forms of plagiarism which are motivated by an intention to cheat, and can presumably only be an enabling factor. After all, typing material from a plagiarised source by hand may require greater effort than copying and pasting, but is still less strenuous than composing an assignment autonomously, and if it is easier for the student to find sources from which to copy, Google makes it equally easy for the teacher to find them.

However, a number of less direct relationships between electronic media and textual plagiarism have been demonstrated or plausibly suggested. Ellery (2008a) found that the preponderance of writers who plagiarised had done so from Internet sources. However, she also found that they were more likely to make notes from print sources than from electronic ones, and points out that note-taking requires some degree of engagement with the source text, while copying and pasting do not. It may not be cheating which electronic media facilitate, but an absence of the critical attention which, when present, leads to good source use.

The status of web-based texts may also be an issue for some students. At the very pragmatic end of the spectrum of potential problems, Ashworth, Freewood and Macdonald (2003) report a student who had a strong determination to avoid plagiarism but was worried that it was possible to plagiarise inadvertently. In this student's view, avoiding plagiarism was all about providing references, and the referencing conventions for web-based materials are less straightforward than those for printed texts, making mistakes in referencing – and thus, as he saw it, plagiarism – more likely.

If it is more difficult to reference electronic sources than print ones, it is due in part to the fact that much of the information which is included in a conventional reference – author, title, date, page numbers – can be missing. Students may have a sense that a web page does not have the same proprietorial status as a book or research article (Bloch, 2001), and if so, they may be right. It is hard to argue that the multiple authors and editors of a Wikipedia article, people who are not credited in the article and may only be identified by pseudonyms if they are searched for, deserve acknowledgement for their unique creative work in the same way that Dickens does for *Great Expectations.* The hypertextual links among web resources contribute additionally to making 'the role of the author rather murky for students' (Belcher, 2001: 142).

The special status of electronic texts appear complex and not always intuitive to teachers (Bloch, 2012); for example, photocopying an article and distributing it to a class may be allowed under 'fair use' rules while e-mailing an electronic version of the same article to the class may not. It is reasonable to think that students are no less likely to be puzzled by these complexities, and this may add to overall uncertainties about which sources to acknowledge, and how and when and why.

Strategies and skills for reading, writing and studying

Bennett (2005) found a relationship between poor study skills and self-reported plagiarism behaviour, and Ashworth, Bannister and Thorne (1997) suggest at least one mechanism for this: students may take notes as they read which inadequately distinguish between ideas from a source and their own thoughts on the source, so that when the notes are later used as a basis for writing, what are effectively unsignalled quotations from the source may creep into the student assignment. A similar explanation was implied by a postgraduate student in the UK in commenting on passages of repeated language in a draft of her MA dissertation:

> if possible, you know, when I finish all the writing and when I feel more confident about what I'm writing I might be able to adapt some of them [extracts from the source] into kind of paraphrasing. . . . so I might be able to do that at the end, do the revision part.
>
> (Pecorari, 2008a: 111)

For this student, copying source language into the dissertation was apparently a conscious and normal part of the writing process, and the time for formulating original wordings and paraphrases was during revision. However, it seems more than possible that when the time for revision comes around, the student may have lost sight of which chunks had been copied from the source and needed paraphrasing.

Paraphrasing from a source, summarising it, or in some other way reformulating it presupposes a number of things on the part of the student: it requires the time and willingness to do so and the awareness of what needs to be paraphrased. It also requires that the student have understood the source, as well as possessing sufficient linguistic resources to find an equivalent formulation. In other words, demands are made on the student's skills in both reading and writing. Difficulties at this stage in the process have been linked to textual plagiarism by a range of researchers. A participant in Shelly Angélil-Carter's classic study of plagiarism worried that 'if I put it in my own words then it's not going to give the same meaning' (2000: 98). Students who, rightly or wrongly, are not confident of their abilities to understand the source, or to rephrase its ideas, have a strong motivation for repeating from it directly.

Learning the rules of the game

A distinctive feature of academic writing is that it is heavily intertextual; most academic genres make frequent reference to other, earlier texts. Avoiding plagiarism can therefore not be accomplished simply by avoiding using other texts at all; the challenge for novice writers is to learn to use sources, but to do so appropriately. However, this involves understanding a complex set of rules for source use, which many students report they lack. A respondent in

Ashworth, Bannister and Thorne's study reflected on the early days of university study:

> It's difficult when you start out in academia. . . . So when I first started I was again unsure about what to do in terms of references and that sort of thing. So you could say that in some of my essays I did things wrong unknowingly because I didn't reference it right. But that was something to do with my lack of experience in academia.
>
> (1997: 192)

The process of learning how to use sources may be an uneven one, and along the way students may develop ideas and conceptions with which their teachers and other gatekeepers would not agree. Ellery (2008b) documented a range of such beliefs, including the idea that a source need only be cited once, and that quotation marks were unnecessary if the source of a quotation were named. A similar idea was expressed by a participant in another study:

> As long as you give the source – showing it's not your work – it's OK even if you copy a paragraph – sometimes you modify more, other times less – depending on your circumstances. The key is you give source and show it's others' work or results, not yours.
>
> (Flowerdew and Li, 2007: 453)

These students had 'learned' facts with which many gatekeepers would not agree; more widely agreed-upon rules are that quotation needs to be signalled by quotation marks (or offset margins or some other similar device) and that simply naming the source is not an adequate signal of quotation. If a source is drawn on multiple times in a text, it may require multiple mentions.

The 'rules of the game', what academic conventions say about how source use should be signalled, is a considerable body of knowledge (Chapter 4 describes it in more detail). It is not surprising if students have misconceptions about it. It should be noted, though, that these 'rules' represent just one area of source use, the declarative knowledge of a set of facts.

Learning to play the game

Beyond the possession of facts, there is also a need for procedural and conditional knowledge: the 'how to' and 'when to' skills. A student who knows to place quotation marks around language repeated from a source does not necessarily know how to avoid quotation by paraphrasing, or when a quotation is more or less appropriate than a paraphrase. A piece of information frequently offered to students is that no citation is needed for information which can be considered common knowledge (Chapter 10 explores this idea in greater depth). However, a student who knows this fact may not have the skills to distinguish between an idea which is common knowledge and one which is not, and requires a citation.

> Learning how to reference is, in the words of a student, a 'hard-won competence', and one he was not sure he had fully mastered. He was worried about his own ability to avoid plagiarism, 'convinced that plagiarism can happen by accident. People can reference inadequately through lack of skill'.
>
> (Ashworth, Freewood and Macdonald, 2003: 268)

Many students arrive at university without significant previous experience in the sorts of skills which are required to use and report sources according to academic conventions. This may be because their earlier writing experience has been with narrative and personal response tasks which did not require them to develop skills in citing sources (Bloch, 2001; Ellery, 2008a) or because they come from educational systems based on lectures and exams, with little or no assessment writing (Timm, 2007a and 2007b; Pecorari, 2008a).

With writing, as with any skill, possessing knowledge about how it is to be done is a necessary but not a sufficient condition. As anyone knows who has ever tried to master a complex skill such as riding a horse or playing tennis or driving a car, simply possessing declarative knowledge about the skill does not guarantee good performance. Indeed, if it did, coaches and teachers would not be needed. Their reminders of 'keep your heels down' or 'don't charge the net' or 'signal before pulling out' would not be needed, at any rate. Novice riders need to be reminded to keep their heels down, but not because they do not *know* that they are supposed to, the reminder is necessary because they *forget* to do so, and one reason they forget is because they must simultaneously remember to do a number of other things, such as keeping their backs straight, their shoulders back, and their hands just above the horse's withers. The reminders will be needed until these procedural skills have become automatised; i.e., until they can be performed automatically, without conscious thought.

Novice riders also often hear that they should 'shorten up the reins', and while the need for this reminder may also depend on the process of adjusting the reins not having been automatised, it may also be caused by a lack of conditional knowledge. It is not the case that reins should always be short; they should be relatively short when more control is needed, and longer when less is needed. Procedural knowledge is knowing when to apply the 'short rein' rule. Thus students who understand what plagiarism is often still have difficulty acting on that knowledge in order to avoid it (Breen and Maassen, 2005) and instructing students in good source use practices (i.e., providing declarative knowledge about how to use sources) can improve their performance, but it does not eliminate problems altogether (Ellery, 2008b; Klitgård *et al.*, 2010).

An additional layer of complexity arises because many of the issues around what can and cannot be done with sources are considerably more complex than keeping your heels down, or keeping your eye on the ball. A case in point is, again, the question of common knowledge. In writing handbooks and plagiarism guides it is easy to find the assertion that no reference is needed for common knowledge. However, what precisely constitutes common knowledge can be unclear to students and teachers both (Errey, 2002) – not because they are uninformed about the principles for good source use, but because the concept genuinely is complex and highly contingent.

If common knowledge is understood to mean facts that 'everybody knows' (as it is frequently defined), then the onus is placed on the student to know what facts everyone else knows. If it is interpreted to mean knowledge which is held in common by the writer and the anticipated reader (Pecorari, 2008b) then the ability to make predictions about the information needs of the reader is required. The ability to predict the response of a specific or hypothetical reader is central to good writing, but it is difficult to acquire. Questions like this, which cannot be answered with a simple, clear-cut rule, make it difficult for students to understand how they are to use sources, and, as Chapter 4 discusses, the act of including a reference in a new text so that the two fit together makes significant demands on the linguistic skills of the writer.

Learning the parlance of the game

Another expectation of academic texts is that they will be, well, academic in tone. Yet usually this does not come easily. As Bourdieu and Passeron have observed, academic discourse is *'jamais pour personne, même pour les enfants des classes cultivées, une langue maternelle'* [never anybody's first language, not even the children of the cultivated classes – translation mine] (1965: 18).

Imitation is a powerful source of learning, and the desire to acquire an academic voice leads writers to imitate those who have it. This can lead to a writing strategy which is often identified as plagiarism, *patchwriting*: 'copying from a source text and then deleting some words, altering grammatical structures, or plugging in one synonym for another' (Howard, 1999: xvii). Patchwriting is 'a primary means of understanding difficult texts, of expanding one's lexical, stylistic, and conceptual repertoires, of finding and trying out new voices in which to speak (xviii). Sources of patchwriting may be

> uneven reading comprehension: the student doesn't fully understand what she is reading and thus can't frame alternative ways for talking about its ideas. Or the student understands what she is reading but is new to the

discourse. She merges her voice with that of the source to create a pastiche over which she exercises a new-found control.

(Howard, 2001: 1)

Another text-based strategy used by novice writers is a sort of academic-discourse cluedo: they observe the features of published texts and try to work out what underlying rules have led the writers to make the choices they have. For example, Ingrid[ii], a postgraduate at a UK university, explained that she had worked out a guiding principle for knowing what needed a citation. If she reported an original finding from a research article, a citation was needed. If, however, she reported something which she understood was 'background information' in that article – a category which seemed to include virtually anything in the introduction – no citations were needed (Pecorari, 2008a). She said that she had deduced this rule from what she read, and believed that this was how published writers in her field worked. Importantly, she added that she had been applying this rule in her own writing, and since her supervisor had not criticised her source use, she assumed the rule and her application of it were both acceptable.

This points to an additional issue in learning to do academic writing which can lead to textual plagiarism. Ingrid had drawn the wrong conclusions about how the authors she was reading had used their sources, because it is not usually possible to know how sources have been used simply by reading the text that cites them. In order fully to understand the relationship between a new work and the sources it has recourse to, it is necessary to conduct a comparison. However, that is not a normal approach to academic reading. Ingrid's supervisor took part in an interview in which he looked at her writing side by side with her sources. He said in no uncertain terms that her source use was *not* acceptable, but, because he had not made a direct comparison before, he did not realise the writing strategy she had been using.

Karin, a lecturer at another university, recounted a story of a nursing student whose final dissertation was found to contain plagiarism. When confronted with it, the student 'was completely shattered and said "I've been doing this all through my nursing training"'. Contributing to her shock was that staff had given her positive feedback on the high standard of language use in her writing assignments (Pecorari and Shaw, 2012: 156).

The knowledge gap that affects all readers about the way a text has used sources thus works to confuse the process of learning to write from sources in two ways. Inexperienced writers will take their cue from the way they see sources used, but only some aspects of source use are visible. Ingrid could see that in the research articles she read, mentions of other scholars' research findings were followed by references. The rule 'if you report someone else's research findings, cite the source' had been observed, and had left visible traces in the works Ingrid read, and therefore Ingrid could deduce the rule. However, some statements in the same articles were not accompanied by references. It may be thought that the statements which were not referenced did not need to be, for example, because they constituted original observations on the part of the authors. If so, another rule had been observed: 'if you make an original observation, no citation is necessary'. But the observance of that rule left no visible traces about the logic underlying it, and so Ingrid had less information to work on, leading her to infer something different: some *types* of information require no citation, even if they come directly from a source.

The fact that some intertextual relationships are more visible than others creates a knowledge gap for teachers as well as for students. If a student cites relatively old sources, the teacher will be able to see that and comment that there are newer ones which should be cited. But if the student copies a paragraph from a source without citing it, provided the language is not suspiciously elegant or a poor fit for the surrounding text, it may not be obvious to the teacher that textual plagiarism has occurred. Unaware of the problem, the teacher cannot give negative feedback about the textual plagiarism, and the absence of critical comments about source use can cause students to assume that their source use is above criticism.

Learning to be a player

Learning a distaste for plagiarism is part of learning academic values and orientations, part of the process of academic acculturation. In Malcolm Bradbury's classic campus novel *Eating people is wrong*, the central character, Treece, listens to a conference paper and recognises it as plagiarised, something which his 'upbringing' in the academy had trained him to regard as just not on:

> Treece knew that Willoughby was getting all this from a book by Edmund Wilson, and he hoped that Willoughby was at least going to credit his sources (the first thing Treece had been told in the academic world, as a simple freshman, had been: a gentleman always credits his sources).
>
> (Bradbury, 1959: 248)

A central theme in the novel is that, at the time Bradbury was writing, universities were only beginning to become the heterogeneous places they are today. Students – and they were indeed mostly gentlemen – could be assumed to arrive at university with good preparation for the academic literacy tasks with which they would be confronted. Today staff may assume that students know how to use sources, but the students themselves are much less certain (Love and Simmons, 1997).

In a much cited essay on the experience of coming to a US university from China, Fan Shen describes the shift in identity which English academic writing required, in order to follow the dictum of English composition: 'Be yourself'. In order to write good English, I knew that I had to be myself, which actually meant not to be my Chinese self. It meant that I had to create an English self and be *that* self.

(1989: 126)

Fully mastering the discoursal conventions for academic writing requires a shift in perspective and identity to become someone with an audience-appropriate message to convey and a sense of the forms in which academic readers are prepared to receive it. The process which brings about that change is a process of cultivating a new identity, a new self, as Fan Shen explained it, and it is a slow and gradual one, and the skills and proficiencies described above are necessary but not sufficient conditions for it to happen. A case study of a remedial writer in the US found that although she was aware to some extent of the implications of copying, her writing skills were not up to the task of producing an independent summary. As a result, she repeated parts of her source. However, she made some changes, in order to cause her reader to perceive her the way she perceived herself, as a serious academic writer, but one who was not yet fully successful: 'If some parts from there I change a little bit, they know I'm not really that kind of student that would copy, 'cause another student would copy' (Hull and Rose, 1989: 147).

Assessing the causes

Thus far this chapter has presented factors which have been identified as potential causes of plagiarism as if they were discrete phenomena with clear boundaries. In fact, they interact with and merge into each other. Students with weaker reading skills may feel motivated on the one hand to reproduce the language of the source because they understood it poorly and fear distorting it, and on the other hand are likely to have spent more time on the task of reading than stronger students, and therefore look for time efficiencies by borrowing language from the source. Students who have not yet acquired an academic identity may both experience difficulties in producing the texts that are expected of them, and feel that the task of trying is not fully incumbent upon them as outsiders.

This blurring of boundaries is especially real with regard to the distinction between prototypical plagiarism and patchwriting. Students can have an awareness that reproducing part of a source is not best practice, and yet not realise that for many academics it is a violation of an ethical principle. The result is neither purely 'innocent' nor truly an act of conscious wrongdoing.

Understanding the causes of plagiarism is an important element in both prevention and response, and the distinction between deceptive and unintentional plagiarism is especially important, as the two acts deserve fundamentally quite different treatments. Students who intentionally attempt to circumvent assessment by deceiving the examiner about the origin of their work deserve, and should receive, sanctions. Responding to prototypical plagiarism thus involves recognising that the usual and desirable relationship between student, teacher and institution, in which all three are willing collaborators in the project of advancing learning, does not obtain, and invoking a disciplinary mechanism which presupposes a refusal on the part of the student to engage with the academic enterprise. On the other hand, students who engage with that project but do not know how to produce assessment work which meets the examiners' expectations need to learn how to do so. Enabling that learning is the reason academic institutions exist. Responding to patchwriting is thus a matter for pedagogy.

Yet, despite the importance in understanding the causes of plagiarism which these fundamental differences imply, reaching that understanding is very difficult. This is illustrated by two symmetrical responses to student plagiarism often heard from teachers. Those who interpret textual plagiarism as having benign origins frequently say 'they can't have known'. Those who believe dishonesty is involved conclude 'they must have known'. The deduction implied by 'can't' and 'must have' is a token of the fact that any understanding of motivation is ultimately based on inference. This lack of certainty can be very frustrating for the staff who deal with plagiarism.

This uncertainty is something that teachers and other gatekeepers should be quite consciously aware of. An implication of it is that it is necessary to be extremely cautious in imputing that most dangerous of intentions, deception, to any writer. This idea is developed further in Chapter 3.

However, a reluctance to assume guilty intent does not mean that plagiarism can or should be shrugged off. An understanding of the causes of textual plagiarism is helpful in identifying an appropriate response, but a diagnosis of benign causes is not a reason to do nothing at all. Any textual plagiarism is potentially risky for the writer who produces it, and so there is a need to respond to it in a way which draws the student's attention to the problem and to solutions. Outlining approaches to doing this is the task of Chapters 4 and 5.

Activity

An interview study of teacher and student perceptions. Interview a teacher from your institution (but not necessarily from your department or unit) and ask these questions:

- What is your working definition of plagiarism?
- Why do students plagiarise?

- Can plagiarism be unintentional?
- Ask about some of the specific causes discussed in this chapter.

Next, interview a student at your institution (but not one of your own students). Ask the same questions. What themes emerge from these two interviews? What views do the teacher and student share, and what differences are there?

A note about interviewing. Several of the activities in other chapters ask you to conduct interviews as well, and it can be useful if you interview the same people each time (though by no means necessary).

Before you begin the first interview, establish ground rules. For example, do your interviewees want to be anonymous when you write up your answers? If you're reading this book as part of a course, you may need to share your answers with others. What is the likelihood that your respondents may be recognised by someone else, from the responses they give, or from your description of them? Discuss this possibility with them and understand how they would like you to handle it. Are you able to offer your participants confidentiality and anonymity? If not, encourage them to answer your questions generally, without giving specific examples of actual cases they have been involved in.

Questions for reflection or discussion

1 Think about a particular case of plagiarism you've encountered. Can you identify some of the factors which caused it? How did the student account for it? How closely did the student's account match your own perceptions?
2 Of the causes described in this chapter, which have you encountered? Are there some which you believe to be more or less common among your students?
3 What types of evidence point to deceptive intention as a cause of plagiarism? Do they point *only* to deception, or can some of them indicate patchwriting as well?
4 If plagiarism is non-deceptive – that is, if the student did not intend to break rules – then he or she must have intended to follow the rules, but been unable to. Among the students at your institution, what factors might explain patchwriting?

3

How do we manage plagiarism?

Summary

This chapter explores universities' approaches to plagiarism in the form of the policies and procedures used to address it, the ways in which it is discouraged, how it is detected and diagnosed by staff and how the university acts when potential cases of plagiarism are identified. The 'quasi-judicial' approach of many institutions and the frequent emphasis on the breaches of the rules is set against the limited measures taken to improve the use of source materials. The methods used by universities to detect plagiarism and the benefits and risks of these processes are discussed. The actions taken when possible plagiarism is discovered and the challenges for staff and policy makers are described. The conclusions reached are that policies and procedures tend to focus on prototypical plagiarism but that there is a significant need to distinguish between this and patchwriting and measures for dealing with patchwriting need to be enhanced.

After reading this chapter you will have an understanding of the processes used by universities to manage plagiarism and their strengths and weaknesses which should enable you to effectively participate in their application and contribute to their enhancement.

The quotation immediately below describes teachers' perceptions of a distinction between a police-like response to plagiarism and a teacherly one. The second discusses aspects of the latter. From your experience, which of these responses does plagiarism call for? What circumstances make one or the other more appropriate?

The ongoing issues for teachers in plagiarism detection generally relate to their roles and responsibilities. Some are disturbed that they are becoming more 'plagiarism police' than teachers, other are uneasy that the plagiarism administration takes focus away from the teaching and learning relationship. Yet others are concerned about the ways in which the issue of plagiarism in the universities is progressing – more towards a punitive and over-regulated outlook of education rather than a truly educative perspective. Some fear that the widespread use of electronic detection for plagiarism sends the wrong message to students and encourages them to seek 'alternative' technologies to subvert this process.

(Sutherland-Smith, 2008: 185–186)

A pedagogy for plagiarism and referencing needs to begin with negotiation of shared meaning around the intricate problems of definition of plagiarism, in the context of the intensely social nature of language and cognition. It needs to move through the development of policy and demonstration materials as a reference point for practice and mediation within the curriculum. Finally, as the acquisition of academic discourses is often not supported by students' prior literacy practices or approaches to knowledge, and such acquisition can of necessity only occur within the academy, an appropriate pedagogy needs to approach plagiarism and referencing constructively, and developmentally, as a way in to an understanding of the nature of academic discourse and the construction of knowledge.

(Angélil-Carter, 2000: 132)

The overarching purpose of this chapter is to describe the ways in which universities typically address plagiarism, in order to highlight the implications for teaching practice, as well as identifying problem areas which require awareness as a first step toward arriving at better practices. Presenting this description necessarily entails some generalisations, and it is clear that some will be a better fit than others for any individual reader's institutional reality. The details of the specific institution are important, though, since those are the ones teachers must follow. In the activity at the end of this chapter you are encouraged to fill out this composite portrait by investigating the situation in your context.

Efforts to address plagiarism are part of a process which can be described as consisting of four stages: 1) regulation (i.e., the production of definitions, policies and the establishment of procedures); 2) prevention, which often takes the form of information and/or warnings directed at students; 3) detection, which was once a laborious *ad hoc* process but now has been automated and made a routine procedure at many universities; and 4) a response to those cases of (possible) plagiarism which the detection process reveals. This chapter examines each of these four stages in turn, describing the features which commonly characterise them, and discussing the helpful and problematic aspects of each.

Policy and regulation

In the English-speaking world and in much of Europe it is very common for university-wide policies to define plagiarism and set forth the processes which are to be set in motion when a case of (suspected) plagiarism is found. Surveys of policies (Pecorari, 2001; Sutherland-Smith, 2010) have shown that while they vary in terms of level of detail, a common feature is that they tend to draw on legalistic language and describe processes in quasi-juridical terms, speaking of the 'accused', 'due process', and otherwise using terminology which is part of the legal system.

Policies typically include features such as definitions (a selection of which were seen in Chapter 1); examples of specific acts or types of texts which can be involved in plagiarism; details of the processes which staff should use to prevent it or (more commonly) respond to cases which arise; details of the processes to which students will be subject if accusations are brought against them; and the range of punishments which may apply to students who are determined to have contravened university rules by plagiarising.

The documentation relating to plagiarism is often part of larger policies on academic misconduct or academic ethics. These typically cover cheating behaviours not classed as plagiarism, such as bringing disallowed aids to an exam, or fabricating evidence of having taken part in a work placement. In some cases regulations about plagiarism and academic ethics generally are embedded in sets of broader regulations which cover behavioural issues such as whether, where and when alcohol and tobacco may be used on university premises, or even safety information and procedures.

Culwin and Lancaster (2001) distinguish between a proactive and a reactive stance toward plagiarism, and the tone in which many policies are written shows them to be primarily reactive, in that they set forth the rules and procedures which will be brought to bear upon offenders once a violation is suspected. When students are suspected of plagiarism, the stipulated procedure tends to be quasi-judicial. It is common to require that some or all cases be referred to a disciplinary board which will ultimately make the determination about whether a breach of rules has occurred. This has the effect of creating a structure reminiscent of a court of law, with the disciplinary panel taking on the role of judge and the staff member who made the accusation (and who may have been required to prepare a formal, written complaint, supplemented with evidence) in the role of the accuser. Other aspects of courtroom formalities are also typically present, such as the right of students to defend themselves against the accusations, and to have representation to help them do so.

The penalties for students who are found to have plagiarised vary enormously and range from warnings to the lowering of a grade to suspension to expulsion or the withdrawal of a degree. Less frequently there may be a stipulation that the student must attend a workshop or lecture on using sources appropriately. By formal policy or informal practice, some types of plagiarism are regarded as more serious than others, and the harsher penalties are reserved for more serious cases. Some policies, though by no means all, make an attempt to describe the characteristics of more or less serious types of plagiarism, and some advocate a tariff of penalties, a scale intended to facilitate consistently heavier penalties for serious cases and lighter ones for the less offensive cases (e.g. Carroll and Appleton, 2005).

What is worth noting is that university policies proscribe, rather than prescribing. They detail behaviours which are not allowed. If they touch upon the question of what students should do, it is typically to mention (often perfunctorily) the importance of acknowledging sources in order to avoid plagiarism. If they address academic values, it is through negative statements about the values which plagiarism is seen to erode, rather than positive statements about the values academic writing should pursue. Example 1.3 from Chapter 1 illustrates this tendency; it explains that 'plagiarism undermines academic integrity simply because it is a form of lying, stealing and mistreating others'. It is much less typical for policies to affront the matter from a positive perspective and explain (for instance) that providing references for claims facilitates the reader's process of critically evaluating the claim, and critical and independent thought is an important academic value.

At one level this emphasis on prohibition rather than the positive is neither surprising nor problematic. Institutions must have rules, and any regulatory framework needs to contain the ingredients listed above: a definition of acts which constitute transgressions and a set of procedures for handling them, including consequences for the transgressors. However, by treating plagiarism exclusively from this perspective, policies take a narrower view than that adopted by many teachers and students for whom plagiarism is an unsuccessful attempt to use sources, and one aspect of the complex task of academic writing. Hunt (n.d.) notes that

Scholars – writers generally – use citations for many things: they establish their own *bona fides* and currency, they advertise their alliances, they bring work to the attention of their reader, they assert ties of collegiality, they exemplify contending positions or define nuances of difference among competing theories or ideas. They do not use them to defend themselves against potential allegations of plagiarism.

Abasi and Graves' (2008) ethnographic study set in a university environment found that teachers had as their objective to introduce students to the ways of writing which were prized in their academic discipline. However, 'the tone and authoritative stance of the university plagiarism policies created considerable anxiety that seemed to have distracted [students] from the more important aspects of academic writing' (228). Thus, by virtue of this narrow perspective, policies are not only restricted in their applicability to prototypical plagiarism, they may draw attention away from patchwriting as well as good writing skills.

Prevention

While policies define rules and describe the consequences of violating them, material aimed at preventing plagiarism is typically presented to students in the form of guides, information sheets and resource pages, often on the website of a study centre or the university library. Efforts at prevention fall into two broad categories: warning and informing. Warnings draw on discourses of law and ethics, and attempt to deter plagiarism by categorising it as a violation of rules, as morally wrong, and as an act which can incur severe penalties.

A subcategory of warning strategies involves asking students to attest in some way that they will adhere, or have adhered, to the rules. This can come in the form of an honour code or code of conduct signed at the beginning of a course of study and/or an assignment cover sheet certifying the work as free of plagiarism.

Informative approaches tend to focus on knowledge about referencing. A typical example appears on the site of a Canadian university[iii]. Headed 'How not to plagiarize', the two-page document (in its PDF form) begins with a quotation from the university's regulations. It then proceeds, in three paragraphs written in an informal and accessible style, to make the connection between disciplinary offences and documenting sources, raising the subjects of the reasons sources are cited in academic writing and referencing conventions. This is followed by five bullet points which pose common questions about source use and then answer them. The last of these questions is 'so what exactly do I have to do to document?' and the 440-word answer offers three categories of material that need referencing and examples of how to produce mechanically correct references according to various common formats. Links to further information are also provided.

What can be noted about these prevention strategies is that they all have the intended effect of raising student awareness of plagiarism as an issue. All other things being equal, awareness should be a positive first step in educating students to avoid plagiarism, and there is some evidence to suggest that this is the case. A survey of students before and after the introduction of a university policy requiring the use of cover sheets (Sims, 2002) found that students became more critical in their attitudes toward various acts identified as plagiarism, and this may indicate that they also became less likely to engage in those acts.

These approaches to prevention are thus not bad in and of themselves, but they have limitations which mean that they are also not sufficient. If a student is not certain what plagiarism is (and as Chapter 1 showed, even their teachers frequently are not), signing a cover sheet certifying an assignment to be free from plagiarism shows little more than good intentions. There is also a question about how many students are reached by warnings. Because plagiarism is characterised as a norm-defying behaviour, students who perceive themselves as honest and rule-abiding may not see that warnings apply to them. The more strident the warnings, the greater the risk that students who have no transgressive inclinations will tune out.

Yet another important limitation is that measures such as the ones described above provide only declarative knowledge about plagiarism and source use. Yet as was seen in Chapter 2, the ability to use sources effectively and appropriately also requires procedural and conditional knowledge. These approaches to prevention can at best hope to keep students from daring to plagiarise and from being unaware that acknowledging sources is important. They cannot aspire to provide a cure for patchwriting.

Detection

While plagiarism is nothing new, the way it is detected has undergone a revolution. As recently as the mid-1980s an academic could describe the detection process like this:

> There is, first, the moment of suspicion, reading along in a student's paper; then the verification of the hunch, the tracking down of the theft, most exhilarating when it involves a search through the library stacks; then the moment of 'confrontation' when the accusation is made and it is no longer the student's paper but his face which is read for signs of guilt, moral anguish, contrition, whatever.
>
> (Hertz, 1985: 148)

Today, though, the hunt for sources which indicate plagiarism increasingly dispenses with the 'search through the library stacks' and involves text-matching software, products which are often referred to somewhat inaccurately as 'plagiarism-detection tools'. Teachers who use such products upload, or have their students upload, assessment work to a server. The student work is then compared to other texts from which it may be plagiarised. Comparisons are typically carried out against texts from three sources. One is anything on the open Internet; that is, web pages which are freely accessible, not password-protected, and do not require a subscription to access. Another is student work submitted at the same time or earlier. Assignments which are submitted become part of the service's database, and therefore become part of the pool of potential sources for the next round of uploaded assignments. Finally, if the service provider has reached an agreement with closed databases or publishers of materials such as electronic books or academic journals, those will be compared. After the process of comparison has been completed, the teacher and/or the student receives a report saying whether the assignment was matched to any possible sources, usually showing the source(s) identified, and providing some sort of quantitative measure of the number of words shared by the student assignment and the putative source(s).

The advantages these products are said to offer range from helping maintain educational standards to saving teachers time to improving the quality of student work itself. The website of one such product, Turnitin, says that it 'improves the student writing cycle by preventing plagiarism and providing rich feedback to students' (Turnitin, n.d.). A competitor states that 'URKUND is an excellent way of adding to the quality assurance of an education' and that 'The teachers do not have to manually check documents for plagiarism or track down sources. Instead they save valuable time' (URKUND, n.d.).

There is no doubt that a computer can compare texts to each other much more quickly than a human can, so if there are comparisons to be made, there are also potential time savings. Or to turn it around, since time is less of the essence, more comparisons can be made. In the days when identifying the sources of a plagiarised work meant hunting through the library, it was done only when a suspicion had arisen. Automatising the process of comparison means that those teachers or institutions which use comparison software frequently run routine comparisons of all submitted assignments.

However, these products, like all things, have the defects of their merits, and these are compounded by unrealistic expectations on the part of the users, or by the law of unintended consequences (Hayes and Introna, 2006). While the automatised comparison of texts is far more systematic and quicker than a manual comparison could be, the process is not fully automated (nor could it be). Work needs to be uploaded for comparison; reports need to be downloaded; work found to have matched one or more possible sources must be checked by the teacher, who needs to decide whether the relationship is an appropriate one. Despite considerable efforts on the part of their producers, comparison tools cannot always distinguish between language which has been copied without acknowledgement and language which has been signalled as quotation; this is a task for the teacher. In these and other ways, comparison tools require the expenditure of teacher time. In an analysis of the use of such products, Culwin and Lancaster conclude that

> Any department considering the introduction of a pro-active policy [using text comparison tools] must take care to compare the costs incurred, primarily valuable staff time, with the benefits obtained, mainly ensuring that only students doing their own work receive academic credit.
>
> (2001: 39)

Text-comparison tools are not magic bullets, then, so the choice to use them or not involves a cost-benefit analysis. The potential benefit identified above – making sure that credit is only received where it is due – depends on the effectiveness of the tools both at identifying plagiarism and at deterring it. In a multi-year study of plagiarism rates at a university which was implementing a text-comparison tool, detection rates were found to fall in the second year, a finding which the authors suggest indicates the tool was having a deterrent effect, although the authors acknowledge that the decrease was not statistically significant (Badge, Cann and Scott, 2007). However, they also note that the product they tested 'does not always detect copying from peer-reviewed subscription journal articles' (437) and this is often the case. Other sources which comparison tools will not ordinarily access include 'paper mills' or 'cheat sites' which sell assignments to students, and which do not allow access to the content until the fee has been paid.

'False negative' results (that is, a report suggesting that an assignment was entirely 'original' when it fact it contained textual plagiarism but the sources were not found) can also be caused because the comparison conducted is at the word level. A student who appropriates an idea for an assignment, or who writes a literature review by using the sources in somebody else's literature review rather than conducting a proper literature search, or who inappropriately re-uses any of the many things which the definitions in Chapter 1 said can be plagiarised apart from words, will not be detected.

Thus, while there are potential benefits to using these tools, there are also limits on their utility. How do the costs weigh up? Culwin and Lancaster were quoted above as saying that the primary cost is teacher time, but there is also the cost of buying in comparison services, separately or in conjunction with a learning platform. Given the financial pressures under which most institutions of higher education labour, the financial costs can only be meaningfully weighed up by setting them against what else could be funded with the same money. To be good options, text-comparison tools need not only to provide a helpful means of providing some information about submitted work; the time a teacher spends using them needs to be more beneficial than if the same time had been spent on writing conferences, or offering an extra tutorial on source-use skills.

Another set of costs which must be weighed are the pedagogical ones: what lessons do we teach students when we use text comparison software? As already noted, some comparisons will result in a false negative result. If the work involved was deceptive plagiarism, then the student will escape the consequences, and that is unfortunate. The consequences are still more unfortunate if patchwriting was involved. As was noted earlier, students who feel uncertain that they know how to use sources often make their best effort and count on getting feedback if they got it wrong. If a text-matching tool discovers no problem, students will understand that to be confirmation that there really was no problem.

There may also be an effect by which feedback is lost. Before comparison tools existed, experienced teachers kept a weather eye out for potential source use problems when they read student work. Teachers who have outsourced the detection of plagiarism to software may assume that they no longer need to be concerned about detection, and may miss problems which should be caught.

The pedagogical lesson involved in routinely scrutinising all student work to see if it violates rules may also offer students a subtext not of their teachers' conscious choosing. The teacher may intend routine checks to signal something like this: 'the work of the honest students is so valuable to me that I will leave no stone unturned to eliminate the possibility that their accomplishments are tarnished by dishonest students'. However, the message received by students may be something entirely different; for example, that students are so dishonest as a group that their work is always and automatically suspect. An interview study asked about automated detection systems and got this response from one participant:

> the student initially took this software to be an aid to student referencing. If work were to be scanned by anti-plagiarism software, that would make apparent the rules of referencing and would be beneficial to the student. But, on being told by the interviewer that the software was intended as a detection device rather than a pre-submission check for the student to ensure referencing was right, this led to change in attitude. He was shocked by the idea. It would distort the process of marking so that it would become policing of plagiarism rather than assessing the student's grasp.
>
> (Ashworth, Freewood and Macdonald, 2003: 269)

In fact, one possible message embedded in routine and systematic checking is that textual plagiarism is such a very bad thing that it outweighs any accomplishments on the part of the student, making it pointless to assess student work until the risk of plagiarism has been eliminated. Once again, that is a much more reasonable response to prototypical plagiarism than to patchwriting. If a student has purchased an essay from a cheat site, then there can be no meaningful assessment of it. But if a student has conceived of an idea and identified evidence and sources of information and fundamentally built an original structure but furnished it with paragraphs borrowed from the sources, then the patchwriting needs a response, but so do the aspects of the work which are positive.

A final lesson which may unwittingly be taught by the use of text comparison tools is that academics are inconsistent and unclear in their beliefs about intellectual property rights. As noted above, student work which is submitted to a comparison service ordinarily is added to the database and becomes a potential source against which future work is compared. The size of the database is an important selling point for these tools. Turnitin describes its database as 'vast', saying that it contains 'over 250 million papers . . . Each day, the Turnitin student database grows by 150,000 papers'. Students who submit their work to Turnitin are therefore contributing to its financial success, without any financial consideration accruing to them. However, the choice to do so is rarely a free one for students; universities or individual teachers who routinely use text-comparison tools typically require submission to the service as a precondition for work to be assessed, and student requests that their work not be archived by the service after the comparison has been conducted have not always been respected (e.g., Glod, 2007). Any valid objection to plagiarism must be based on the idea that there is such a thing as an original creation, and the rights of the creator must be respected by, at a minimum, appropriate acknowledgement. To sacrifice the intellectual property rights of students in order to combat plagiarism is an oddly inconsistent position for academics to adopt.

Response

In responding to plagiarism teachers at many institutions are bound to follow procedures specified by policy. For example in Sweden, the regulations which govern higher education, and which have the force of law, stipulate that anyone who has a well founded suspicion that a student has attempted to deceive during the course of assessment must report that 'expeditiously to the Vice Chancellor' (HSF 1993: 100. Chapter 10, paragraph 9). Even if a teacher is not bound to follow a certain course of action, institutional support is likely to be available only for the type of response that official policy specifies. It is therefore only possible to generalise about a response to plagiarism at the policy level.

At that level, though, many teachers feel dissatisfied or let down. Stipulations of official policy may seem unrealistic, making it impossible or impracticable to follow them uniformly. In a response to a survey of plagiarism policies internationally, an Australian academic first described the policies in place at his university but then added 'while the penalties seem very harsh, and they have been invoked, the way in which they are run depends very much on the level of the student in the system. . . . I would leave most of the issues . . . to be dealt with by my tutors and not involve the university at all' (Pecorari, 2001: 232–233). This view was shared by the Australian teachers Sutherland-Smith interviewed, who said that it was better 'if cases of plagiarism are handled by teachers and not through formal academic processes' (2005: 93). In a North American study, Abasi and Graves found that

> most faculty members complied [with policy] by copy-pasting a section from the university brochure or by incorporating the URL of the electronic version of the brochure in their course outlines. They did so, however, with a large degree of discomfort as they believed that including these admonitions about plagiarism interfered with their pedagogical goals.
>
> (2008: 229)

Another respect in which teachers may feel unsupported by policy is at the point of deciding what action is needed and when. The usefulness of policy as a guide for action stands or falls on the strength of the definitions of plagiarism associated with them. Definitions, as noted in Chapter 1, are a common feature of plagiarism policies, but they are written in general and abstract terms. When teachers are confronted with student assessment work which may be plagiarised, they struggle to apply the definitions, asking themselves questions such as whether someone else's words have been taken and used, or whether similarities are coincidental; or whether an idea is common knowledge or requires a citation (Pecorari and Shaw, 2012). Whether the procedures specified in a policy need to be invoked depends in part on whether the teacher believes the offence of plagiarism as defined in the policy has been committed, and crossing the gap between a theoretical understanding of the definition and applying it in practice is difficult.

When a decision has been made to report a case of plagiarism, teachers often report feeling exposed. The additional work involved in detecting plagiarism and preparing a case for the disciplinary board can be considerable. If the teacher believes a student to be guilty of plagiarism – which is likely if a formal report was made – but the decision of the ethics board, academic standards officer or other relevant authority is different, then feelings of exposure can turn into frustration. Teachers may feel undermined or even victimised by the institutions they work for, and whose rules they were trying to uphold (Bretag, 2004; Sutherland-Smith, 2005). There may also be a sense that the decision constituted criticism, implied or explicit, of their handling of the issue.

It is perhaps inevitable that many of these difficulties should exist. The adage that hard cases make poor law may have a parallel here, at least as far as deceptive plagiarism goes. As a form of cheating, a violation of a rule which exists to protect certain institutional ideals, plagiarism will always be a 'hard case'; that is, it constitutes a problem to solve outside of the usual mechanisms and processes of normal academic activity. If plagiarism cases occurred and were detected and reported only rarely, then the less than smooth working of the mechanisms to deal with it would have minimal impact in the large picture.

Most of the problems raised in this chapter come about, though, first because plagiarism is not a rare phenomenon, and second because it frequently occurs in a non-deceptive form. Patchwriting is the evidence of as-yet incomplete learning attainments, and as such it requires a pedagogical response. However, the institutional procedures typically in place are tailor-made for prototypical plagiarism, and ill suited for dealing with patchwriting. The problem is thus not primarily with the procedures themselves; problems arise when the procedures are applied to cases for which they are a poor fit. In order to deal effectively with patchwriting, a parallel set of measures with a focus on teaching and learning, rather than detection and punishment, are needed. Describing them is the task of the next two chapters.

Activity

A report on procedures and how they are explained. Start by reflecting on how you would handle a case of plagiarism if you discovered one. What do the policies and procedures at your institution say?

- If you think you know, describe what you understand to be the correct procedure, and then consult the relevant sources of information to see if your understanding was correct.
- If you're not sure, find that information and then describe it.

Then consider these questions:

- Where and how was information about handling plagiarism available? How did you go about finding it?
- How do the procedures specified match what staff actually do in your experience?

Questions for discussion or reflection

1 This chapter characterised many plagiarism policies as engaging in a discourse of legality and/or morality. Is this true for your university's policy? If so, what language supports that conclusion? If not, how would you characterise its tone?

2 If you have had the experience of reporting a case of suspected plagiarism to a disciplinary authority, what was the outcome? Were you satisfied with the outcome? Were there aspects of the case which you think were not fully understood by the body which made the decision?

3 This chapter quoted a student as perceiving that text-comparison software was a 'policing' effort with which he was uncomfortable. Are there ways of introducing the use of such software to students without provoking that response?

4 In a report on a trial at her university using Turnitin, Emerson (2008) illustates the issues by drawing a parallel between the student experience of plagiarism and her experience with an aspect of crossing cultures. As a New Zealander travelling to the US, she struggled to come to grips with customs for tipping in restaurants, and despite her best efforts, knew that she did not always get it right. She considers what the same level of partial failure would mean for a student struggling with rules for source use:

> Had I known that moral censure, personal and family shame, and failure to achieve lifelong dreams might ensue from a single error in grasping these culturally determined practices, then the stress would have been considerably higher. I wanted to be able to tip – it wasn't that I didn't care or didn't try. But I sometimes failed out of frustration at my inability to grasp the complexities. If we had added to the situation a device that would unerringly detect every error I made, I would probably have taken the safe route (McDonald's every day?) or tipped excessively at every possible moment.
>
> (2008: 192)

For students learning to use sources, what is the equivalent of 'the safe route', the 'McDonald's every day' option? If taking the 'safe route' causes students to avoid textual plagiarism, is it problematic if they follow it? Why or why not? Emerson implies that 'moral censure, personal and family shame, and failure to achieve lifelong dreams' might be the consequence if a student makes a mistake with plagiarism as she did with tipping. Is that too dramatic a view of the situation, or is it realistic?

Part Two

Managing plagiarism

4

What do writers need to know to avoid plagiarism?

Summary

This chapter explores patchwriting, i.e. the inappropriate use of sources resulting from limitations in the student's knowledge or writing skills. The solution is to give the student the information he or she needs and the opportunities to develop and practice the skills required to use and cite sources appropriately. The principles that source use should be transparent to the reader and sources should serve as a necessary function in the text are discussed. Three aspects of transparency are set forth: reporting content from the source transparently; identifying the sources which have informed the new text; and indicating the source of the language used. Examples are provided to illustrate good and less good practices. While the use of the principles and practices provided should enable the reader to avoid plagiarism, it is acknowledged that further development will be required to enable the reader to develop the knowledge and skills required to become a proficient academic writer.

When you have finished this chapter you will be aware of key principles and the specific skills which apply to the use of sources and be able to convey that understanding to your students.

Consider the ideas expressed in the quotations below about successful and unsuccessful source use. Are they fundamentally in agreement or disagreement?

Quotation, paraphrase, incorporation, argumentation, influence, and provision of support and authority: all of this is supposed to occur in citations, even while students acknowledge the point of the class for which the assignment is due, indicated that they have done class readings and more, and demonstrate that they have their own original perspective, different from everyone else's, including the experts. References are where the academic action is, and quotation with proper citation is the proof that a student has joined the club. When students fail at some aspect of this daunting task – when they consult outside works but neglect to cite them correctly – they are accused of committing plagiarism. Even in the best of situations, this is a skill that cannot be learned without meticulous attention. . . .

(Blum, 2010: 40)

Immature poets imitate; mature poets steal; bad poets deface what they take, and good poets make it into something better, or at least something different. The good poet welds his theft into a whole of feeling which is unique, utterly different from that from which it was torn; the bad poet throws it into something which has no cohesion.

(Eliot, 'The Sacred Wood', 1920)

This chapter is concerned with the sort of plagiarism that occurs when a writer is willing to follow rules but unable to write in the way the rules prescribe, i.e., patchwriting. This sort of textual plagiarism is caused by limitations on the writers' knowledge and/or skills, and the solution to it is to teach students the things they need to know, and the things they need to be able to do. In this sense, the problem is not really one of avoiding plagiarism but of learning to write well from sources, so that plagiarism becomes a non-issue. Although handling prototypical plagiarism, the deceptive kind, is not primarily the subject of this chapter there are nonetheless relevancies for it. Chapter 2 showed that the causes for cheating include pressures which lead students to believe that there is no other alternative, and that justifications for cheating can be found. Students who possess the necessary knowledge and skills to produce sound academic texts will, presumably, be less likely to feel that either the pressures or the justifications apply.

The focus in this chapter is on what the writer needs to know (while Chapter 5 addresses how it can be delivered). However, in a sense explaining all that a writer needs to know about using sources is an impossibly ambitious enterprise. To be able to write an academic text which makes appropriate and effective use of its sources, a writer needs to have identified sources which can inform the subject at hand, and have read and understood not just their content, but how they relate to the current topic, to each other, to the existing body of literature on the subject, and to key concepts in the area. The writer must then be able to construct a strong text with an original idea at its heart, and draw on sources which make relevant contributions to illuminating that idea. Depending on disciplinary practices this can involve an elaborate network of carefully crafted quotations, paraphrases and summaries or a spartan restatement of facts with straightforward numbered references, but in either case the writer needs both the disciplinary knowledge of what is required and the rhetorical abilities to deliver it.

In short, to produce work characterised by appropriate source use, student writers need to become mature, experienced writers in their area of study, requiring subject-specific knowledge and skills. While this specific knowledge is something that can only be learned within the context of the subject curriculum, some general principles can guide that learning, and those are the focus of this chapter. The activity at the end of the chapter will add further detail to this picture from the perspective of the individual reader's context. The application of these principles should shorten the student's journey to a sound landing place. Once there, the student should have good preconditions for developing the skills and techniques of mature academic writing.

This description of the principles that underlie good source use and thus permit students to avoid plagiarism takes a conservative approach. Given the diversity of views which exist about what, specifically, constitutes plagiarism, it is a virtual certainty that some readers will think this approach is too conservative, and will believe that it blocks the use of some writing strategies which are legitimate, at least in some circumstances. The rationale for approaching the question with an extra grain of caution is precisely this diversity of views. Students need to know what they can do to be safe from the accusation of plagiarism. Achieving that safety means remaining above all serious criticism. Producing work which a given teacher deems acceptable is not enough; students need the ability to write texts which *no* gatekeeper could reasonably call plagiarism.

Transparency

An essential principle guiding all appropriate source use is that the ways in which sources have informed the new text should be transparent for the reader. That is to say, the impression a reader forms about how sources have been used should be the correct one. A corollary of this principle is that it is the writer's responsibility to make sure that transparency is achieved. The reasons for this lie in the nature of academic writing. While academic texts are meant to contain something that is original, they are not exercises in creative writing; the original contribution must be contextualised in the existing literature in the area. A piece of writing which failed to take note of what has already been done on a topic would be fundamentally unacademic. Thus academic writing is 'multi-voiced' – the voice of the writer is joined by the voices of the authors of the sources he or she cites, and the readers of academic texts need to be able to distinguish their individual contributions. As Groom puts it, 'it is a conventional expectation among readers of all but the most playfully postmodern of Anglophone academic texts that it will be clear at any given point whose "voice" is "speaking"' (2000: 15).

This creates the demand for transparency; the need for the writer to take responsibility for ensuring transparency comes about because so much about the ways that sources are used would be hidden from the reader's view if the writer did not assume that responsibility. This can be illustrated with reference to the quotation immediately above. The fact that it is recognisable as a quotation at all is because of the devices used to signal it, which include quotation marks, the name of the author, a year identifying which of the author's publications the quotation is from, and the number of the page on which it is found. If these were missing, few readers would be likely to understand that that paragraph drew upon any sources at all. (If any did, it would be because they had themselves read that source and retained a sufficiently clear memory of it to make the connection.)

Importantly, because the reader usually cannot see how sources have been used without the writer's help, achieving transparency rests not only on the writer's willingness and ability to signal the real relationships between the new text and its sources, it also depends on the reader's ability to interpret the signals. Most readers will have drawn certain inferences about the end of the last paragraph but one: that the statement beginning with 'it is a conventional' and extending as far as 'speaking' appears in another work, worded in that way; that the author of the work was called 'Groom'; that the work was published in 2000; that, if the reference list is consulted, full bibliographical details of the quoted work can be found; and that the quotation appears on page 15 of that book.

If those are the inferences you drew, you are correct, but they were inferences; the only way you could be certain would be to turn to the references at the end of this book, and, using the bibliographic information there, find the source and check. The noteworthy point is that the accuracy of the inferences depends on the use and understanding of rather compact signals. The five inferences listed above, which took 62 words to spell out, are actually signalled in the text by nothing more than a name, two numbers and a few punctuation marks.

Readers may have drawn other inferences as well. The reference to Groom was the first citation to another source in this chapter, so if you stopped to think about it, you may have concluded that I am asserting that the other ideas up until that point are mine; that I am *averring* them, claiming them as true on my own authority, rather than *attributing* them to another author, to use Tadros' (1993) distinction. Averral is the default assumption in academic writing, and is not explicitly signalled at all; the way we know a writer is averring an idea is that the writer does not use any signals to indicate attribution.

In this case the accuracy of the inference depends as well on a shared understanding of what it means for an idea to need, or not need, attribution. For instance, the idea that academic writing is 'multi-voiced' in the sentence preceding the quotation to Groom is one which I feel comfortable averring because I know it to be true, of my own experience, and not *because* I read it somewhere, although I have in fact read it somewhere; indeed, many places, and Groom's work is one of them. My belief that I do not need to attribute that idea is based on an understanding that this is a widely accepted fact which has been noted prolifically in my professional literature, and is indeed merely a specific instantiation of the fact that most texts are multi-voiced in the sense that they have intertextual features, as noted by Bakhtin (e.g., 1986) and Kristeva (e.g.,1980), among many others.

My conclusion is that while there are very many names that could be cited for the assertion that academic texts are multi-voiced, the reader would not be well served by a list of them, and the principle of transparently revealing my sources does not require me to cite them, because none of them is directly the source of my assertion: the source of my assertion is my confident understanding of the nature of academic texts. This conclusion is based partly on my reflections about the sources which have influenced me, but also partly on my interpretation about where the boundary between that which can be averred and that which must be attributed falls, and it is possible that some readers may not agree with me. However, without this detailed explanation, it is likely, again, that few readers would be aware of the question at all.

The purpose of this excursion into a specific example of my own citation practices is to illustrate one source of difficulty in putting the principle of transparency into practice: some of the decisions which must be made are highly subjective. This means that the decision I made is not necessarily the one another writer would have made. How challenging is the decision-making for a novice academic writer, who is equipped with less experience as well as less confidence?

Compounding that challenge is the issue noted above, that even where the nature of what is to be signalled is more straightforward, the signals used are small, and compress a great deal of meaning into small symbols, and require interpretation, and all of this means that even when a writer makes a good-faith effort to reveal the ways that sources have influenced the new text, there is room for the signals to be given imprecisely by the writer, or interpreted incorrectly by the reader.

Example 4.1a

Evaluation of a degree programme may be conducted at several different levels – at the level of 'a single teaching episode, at the level of a set of teaching episodes, at the level of a course section/unit, or at the level of the total course.' (Pyle and Sayers, 1980). This study is principally concerned with the last level, and the style of evaluation employed might be broadly described as illuminative. (Parlett and Hamilton, 1972).

Example 4.1a, written by an MA student at a UK university to introduce the work she intended to undertake for her dissertation, illustrates that the relationships signalled by student writers can in fact be misleading. The student appears to combine averral with attribution to two sources, and only a relatively small part of the paragraph is signalled as quotation. A reasonable interpretation of the influence her sources have had on her work is that the large idea that different levels or aspects of education can be evaluated comes from Pyle and Sayers, while the part that is not signalled as quotation is her own wording. In the context of a description of proposed research, 'this study' may be understood to refer to the student's own research, and thus the statement that it 'is principally concerned with the last level' would be an averral, a statement of the intention she has herself developed for her project. The reference to Parlett and Hamilton at the end of the sentence may suggest that they use the term 'illuminative' for the sort of evaluation she proposes.

In fact, as Example 4.1b (taken from Pyle and Sayers) shows, many of these assumptions are wrong. The entire paragraph comes virtually verbatim from Pyle and Sayers, and the reference to Parlett and Hamilton is also taken from them. The comment about 'this study' which appeared to be an averral also comes from that source, though in the original context it referred to Pyle and Sayers' study.

Example 4.1b

Evaluation of a degree programme may take place at several different levels – at the level of a single teaching episode, at the level of a set of teaching episodes, at the level of a course section/unit, or at the level of the total course. This study is principally concerned with the latter two levels, and the style of evaluation used might be broadly described as illuminative (Parlett and Hamilton, 1972).

In an interview about her source use, the writer who produced Example 4.1a made frequent reference to the rules, as she understood them, governing source use, and what she believed was required and prohibited. Getting her source use right was very much on her mind. However, if she had asked a different set of questions – not 'What am I required to do to avoid plagiarism?' but 'What is the best way to help the reader understand what I've done?' – it might have been clearer to her that her referencing was misleading.

The principle of transparency, along with the reasons why it is needed, and why transparency can be so hard to achieve, are things that students need to learn. In addition, they need to learn how to achieve transparency with respect to three features of source use: the content reported; the identity of the source used; and the source of the language in which the content is transmitted.

The identity of the source

The broad principle of transparency says that the reader should be able to understand how sources have informed the new text. As far as the identity of the source, this means that they should understand *which* sources have had an influence. In simplest terms this amounts to saying that writers should acknowledge their sources.

The primary means by which this is done is through some form of in-text reference. These, of course, come in many shapes and sizes. Two different systems were illustrated in Examples 1.4 and 1.5 in Chapter 1, and many others exist; for example, version 3.0 of the Zotero referencing tool offers a menu of 12 styles according to which references can be prepared, including those of the American Psychological Association (APA), the Modern Language Association (MLA) and the Harvard system. Student writers are often asked to adopt one of these conventions, particularly when presenting works which, like dissertations or theses, are expected to reach a relatively high level of formal precision.

Students are often concerned about getting the technical details of these referencing conventions right, and the 'how not to plagiarise' information which many universities offer to students frequently describes these systems and the differences among them in great depth. This may be because the details of referencing systems are thoroughly described (in some cases, exhaustively: the sixth edition of the *APA Publication Manual* runs to 290 pages, a significant proportion of which, approximately 55 pages, is dedicated to in-text referencing, reference list entries, and other aspects of documenting source use). This detail offers a seductive appearance of order and certainty which students and teachers crave.

However, it is important to keep in mind that the details of citation conventions are nothing more than the mechanics of referencing (see also Jamieson, 2008, for a discussion of this point). Getting the mechanics right can be important, but it is a lower-order question than the principle behind the reason the references are there at all, i.e., to ensure that the influences on a text are signalled for the reader to see. Making a mistake about the mechanics of a reference will at worst make the work look sloppy; failing to identify sources which have materially influenced the new work can on the one hand deprive the work of the benefits of effective source use, such as showing that the writer is aware of what has been written on the topic, and may on the other hand be diagnosed as plagiarism.

Although the principle that sources should be acknowledged is a fairly straightforward one, inexperienced writers have difficulty with some aspects of it. An issue which is the source of many student questions is second-hand citation. For example, while preparing an assignment, the writer reads a work by Jones; Jones quotes Smith on a point which the writer wants to cite in her work. Students are often unsure how to do this, and frequently resolve the matter by citing one or the other of the sources: the original and not the work which cites it, or the other way around (the writer in Example 4.1b above did the latter).

There appears to be consensus that second-hand citation is relatively undesirable. One good reason for not citing sources indirectly is to avoid starting a round of the academic equivalent of the birthday-party game 'whispers' (the first person whispers an idea into the ear of the person sitting next to her, and so on, and by the time the message comes full circle, the cumulative effect of the small distortions which were introduced along the way is seen to have changed the message radically). The best alternative under ideal circumstances is to consult the original source, in which case it can be cited directly.

However, going back to the original is not always practically possible. The original may be a book which is checked out from the library or an article from a journal to which the institution does not subscribe, so that by the time it is ordered and arrived the deadline for the assignment has passed. The principle of transparency suggests that the best solution in that case is to use the idea, but to cite it in such a way that the reader understands which sources have actually been used (e.g., 'Smith, as cited in Jones'). In that way the reader is aware of the 'chain of custody' of the idea, and in evaluating it can take into account the fact that Jones may have distorted Smith's idea.

Another potential problem area related to source identity is the ability to gather bibliographic information in order to report the correct information about the source. For example, students who refer to a chapter in an edited volume (or anthology) often cite the editor of the work, rather than the author in question. Example 4.2, also from a draft of an MA dissertation, does precisely this (as well as other things which violate the transparency principle). In this example (and elsewhere) she cites Fullan and Hargreaves, who were the editors of the collection but not the authors of this paper. At one level this is a fairly trivial matter, a mistake which, if made, can easily be corrected. At another level, though, it may be symptomatic of larger problems in understanding the relationship among scholars working within a field, and thus, potentially, the relationship among ideas. Using this approach it would be possible, for example, for a writer to cite diametrically opposed ideas from two different authors in the same collection and attribute them to the same person, the editor.

Example 4.2

Student

An interesting characteristic of culture as Fullan and Hargreaves put it, questions the concretness [*sic*] of the above definition, as they both claim that culture is invisible. However, they do take the argument even further to explain that culture is indeed invisible 'but it is made visible only through its representation' (Fullan and Hargreaves, 58–60).

Source

'Culture is not itself visible, but is made visible only through its representation' (Van Mannen, 1988:3). Culture is constructed reality. It is known by its representation.

To avoid this problem and be able to identify the relevant information about sources, students need to be familiar with the various forms of academic publications, such as journal articles, monographs and anthologies. This is also necessary in order to be able to satisfy the requirement at the purely mechanical level for giving different sorts of bibliographic information for different types of sources. Once that familiarity is gained, though, it will also help students understand the roles that various actors play in creating them, and what that implies for the relationships among works of various types. For example, while the papers in an anthology are typically linked by a very tight theme, the papers in any given issue of a research journal (unless it is a themed issue) are related only by being examples of work within the same broad subject area. Journal articles are generally published more expeditiously than books, so research journals are a good place to look for the latest research findings.

It has been suggested (e.g., Belcher, 2001; Bloch, 2012) that the increasing prevalence of electronic texts, the Internet as a source of information and, concomitantly, hypertext, leads to a situation in which authorship may be increasingly masked, especially for inexperienced academic writers. If so, identifying the identity of sources will become more of a problem over time, rather than less.

A further issue which novice writers in particular find problematic is understanding which sources influenced them directly enough to require a citation. A typical question, and one which reveals a sophisticated understanding of the problem of writing from sources, is along the lines of 'I've read a lot. How do I really know which sources have influenced me?'

The most relevant point about this question is that there is no possible answer which is categorically and unproblematically correct. There are, however, good processes and strategies for trying to find the best possible answer. At the pragmatic end, good note-taking strategies require writers to articulate more consciously what they have learned from which sources. Some understandings, though, come not from reading fact A in source X, but from having read widely and pieced together facts and views in new constellations. This is in fact the best-case scenario, the intended purpose of reading one's way into a new topic.

As the discussion of multi-voiced texts earlier was intended to indicate, this is not a question which has a single right answer. It is a question about which the writer must reflect and reach a decision. This can be frustrating: imagine learning to speak Spanish or do quadratic equations, and attempt an exercise and not be able to check whether the answer was right. However, the process of getting to the best possible answer, of reflecting on the reasons for or against doing it this way or that, raises awareness of the principles which underlie the decisions and is therefore beneficial in itself.

Content from a source

The aspect of transparency which regards the content of the source has two strands to it. The first is that content which derives from a source must be reported accurately. This is not a conceptually difficult principle, but it throws up a number of practical problems. In order to report the propositional content from a source accurately, students must, obviously, understand it. However, the sort of reading which students do at university level is often challenging (and indeed is intended to be, and should be). Further, a thorough understanding of an academic text requires understanding of how the ideas it treats are positioned in relation to others in the same field. Are the ideas it presents established, or does it challenge the received view? Is it a logical outcrop of earlier developments reported in earlier texts? This understanding requires a degree of experience which develops slowly, and which new members of a discourse community cannot be expected to possess.

Another aspect of transparently reporting content is presenting it in terms which tell the reader how it is to be interpreted and used. In Example 4.3 a proposition attributed to Weber is introduced with 'argues', while Krippendorff 'suggests' a different idea. These two verbs convey fundamentally different messages about how the source authors regard the reported ideas. Suggesting that something is true leaves open the possibility that it also may not be, and this degree of hesitance is confirmed later in the example: thematic units '**may** be preferable'.

'Argue', though, carries a different message. First, it gives the impression that Weber's commitment to the proposition is greater than Krippendorff's, because Weber is prepared to put up an argument to defend it. Second, it classifies the proposition as something contentious: there is no need to argue for something which everyone accepts.

Example 4.3

Weber (1990, p. 37) argues that word categories inferred from covariation among high-frequency words are more reliable than themes. However Krippendorff (1980, p. 63) suggests that for many content analyses, thematic units, requiring user judgment in the determination of the hidden messages conveyed in the narratives, may be preferable despite difficulties in application which have restricted the use of this approach to content analysis in practice.

By selecting 'argues' in one case and 'suggests' in the other, the authors of the research article from which this example was taken have made a meta-commentary on the content, but it is one where accuracy is at least as important; to portray an author as having a strong commitment to an idea which he or she only puts forward tentatively, for example, would be as serious a distortion of the source as confusing the facts reported in it.

Reporting verbs not only can indicate what the author thinks of the cited propositions, they allow the writer to evaluate the proposition as well (Thompson and Ye, 1991, call these 'author stance' and 'writer stance' respectively). If the source 'notes' something, that indicates that the writer agrees with it, while 'states' or 'says' withholds this positive evaluation, and words like 'confuses' indicate that the writer thinks the source author was wrong.

In fulfilling the responsibility to report source content transparently, then, writers need not only to be able to understand the source and convey ideas from it in such a way that the propositional content is not distorted, they must also be able to use reporting language in such a way that what the author and the writer think about the content emerges clearly and (in the case of the author's evaluations) accurately.

The source of the language

In reporting material from a source, writers have two choices, to quote it (i.e., to repeat it verbatim and accurately) or to paraphrase, conveying the idea in an original wording. In fact, some researchers in this area distinguish a third option, summary. If this distinction is made, summary is used to indicate a greatly condensed retelling of the large themes in an extended part of the source text, while paraphrase is reserved to indicate a rewording of a specific idea. While this distinction is a valid one, both involve some fundamental transformation of the language of the source while staying faithful to its idea, so for the sake of simplicity, 'paraphrase' will be used here for both sorts of rewordings.

Here too there are some relatively straightforward principles to do with the mechanics which students need to know. These include the ways that minor changes can be made to quotations, such as the use of an ellipsis (. . .) to signal words which have been omitted and square brackets to show that a word has been changed. Other conventions include the need to give a page reference for quotations (in APA style, preceded with 'p.' but not in MLA style) and the use of quotation marks for shorter quotations, while longer quotations are separated from the main text and have narrower margins.

However, here too the mechanics are of less importance than the principle that the reader should be able to make the right inferences about where the language in a text comes from: is it the writer's, or the source's? (This principle can also be seen to shape the mechanical rules. For example, not only must words removed from a quotation be signalled with an ellipsis, if they are removed, it should not have the effect of distorting the meaning, so that the reader gains a misleading impression of what the original said.)

The challenges in realising this transparent relationship are, logically enough, related to language use. Quotation tends to be less problematic, although introducing a quotation so that it fits smoothly into the text around it presents certain rhetorical difficulties. However, paraphrasing poses a linguistic challenge of the highest order: the writer must be able to encapsulate an idea (and, in academic writing, possibly a complex and difficult idea) in language which is both grammatically correct and appropriately academic sounding, without distorting the meaning of the original.

The distinction between paraphrase and quotation is a distinction between two discrete categories; it is not a distinction between two points on a continuum, with other legitimate strategies in between. However, when writers lack confidence in their abilities to produce accurate and appropriate-sounding representations of the ideas in their sources, they often adopt a strategy that is neither quotation nor paraphrase. In Example 4.4 much of this passage from a student text is worded in the same way as the student's source, but she has made some changes: for example, 'has increased significantly in recent years' becomes 'has recently been increased'. This fails to achieve transparency because the changes are clearly just that: the student has taken the language of her source as her starting point and not acknowledged it. Making the changes more thorough-going still would not address the transparency issue, because the nature of the relationship, that the source provided a start on the wording, and not just the propositional content, would not be signalled to the reader.

Example 4.4

Student

Much work has been carried out on the evaluation of INSET in a local, national and international basis, and such work has recently been increased as a result of increasing emphasis on accountability of the provision of INSET.

> **Source**
>
> Much work has been carried out on the evaluation of INSET, on a local, national and international basis; and the volume of this work has increased significantly in recent years as accountability has become more prominent.

This strategy of stitching together elements from one text with elements from another and making some superficial changes to the language is what Howard has called *patchwriting*, and it is very common (Pecorari, 2003; Howard, Serviss and Rodrigue, 2010). It is also probably the aspect of source use which attracts the greatest variation of opinions across disciplines and individually. As Chapter 8 will show, some disciplines make little or no use of explicitly signalled quotation, but may have a greater tolerance for unsignalled near-quotation, and as Chapter 1 discussed, this is a strategy which has been defended as fully legitimate, at least under some conditions, by some academics. However, many others class it as a form of plagiarism, so to be fully safe from accusations of plagiarism, students must have the writing skills which will enable them to abandon patchwriting. This puts an especially heavy burden on students writing in subject areas in which explicitly signalled quotation is not a viable option.

Effective source use

Understanding the principle of transparency and having the skills to act on its implications will keep writers from doing things which can be identified as plagiarism, but adherence to that principle alone will not produce good written assignments, and neither will understanding the principle provide answers to all the questions students have about source use. Another important idea that students need to understand is to do with the role that sources play in the larger purpose of their text.

The first step in this understanding is the realisation that texts should have a purpose. For experienced academic writers this is an obvious assertion. For students who are accustomed to think of writing as something they have to do in order to pass a course, it is less obvious. Having a purpose also implies having something to say, and expecting newcomers to a subject to have things to say about it is a moderately big ask. Writing for assessment means finding something to say about a topic *to the teacher*, who knows much more about the topic than the student does, and that can be a daunting prospect indeed.

In academic writing, the purpose typically is to communicate original content in the context of what is already known about the topic. In the case of research articles, or theses and dissertations, the new content is typically research findings. In assessment writing the new element is likely to be the student's own understanding.

Regardless of the specific purpose of the text, references to sources have an important role but one which is secondary to the main task of the text. In the case of research writing, this includes describing the existing research on the topic, in order to be able to argue for the need for the new work. Reference to sources can also serve functions such as providing support for the writer's assertions, demonstrating that there is a diversity of thought on an issue, etc. The point, though, is that they do have a purpose, a specific role to play. This too may be an eye-opener for students who think of references as a requirement, something to include in a piece of writing to demonstrate the reading that has been done, or simply because everyone else does.

Once in place, this understanding can be a powerful tool for making the decisions which writers must make in using sources transparently. For example, it provides insights into the nature of which sources to use. Not only are web-based sources a potential source of confusion about authorship, as noted above, they are an area that students often ask about. However, questions are often couched in terms which suggest that there are clear rules which can be learned and followed. A typical question might be 'Am I allowed to cite Wikipedia?'. Some teachers have such strong feelings about Wikipedia that they do not allow students to cite it, so a rule-based answer is available there. However, a more helpful response would be to encourage students to think of the choice in terms of the reason they want to cite it. If the purpose of the reference to Wikipedia is to establish that a given fact is true, then there are probably more credible sources available, and the reference will be more effective in accomplishing its purpose if a more authoritative source, instead of Wikipedia, is chosen.

The effectiveness of source use also helps explain why both patchwriting and an excessive reliance on quotation are to be avoided. However close the relationship in terms of topic between the source and the new text, it will not be identical (ideally; asking students to write on topics which have already been addressed in identical form will not encourage them to write independently of their sources, a point which is taken up in the next chapter). An idea from a source most often needs to be worded in a new way to fit into a new text.

A number of questions about source use are genuinely difficult to answer from the perspective of what writers are *required* to do. A case in point is this: 'I had an idea, and then when I was doing a literature search I found the same idea in a source. Do I have to cite the source?' The best answer to this question is usually in terms of what the writer will find it advantageous to do. Even if it is not necessary to credit the source with providing the idea, a reference will provide additional support for it, and thus allow the writer to make the same point more strongly. Reporting language can be used strategically to signal that relationship to the reader as well. 'Smith states . . .' conveys the message that the assertion comes entirely from Smith, and additionally positions Smith as an authority, but 'As Smith notes . . .' places the writer in a position of independent authority; it means something like 'Smith said it, and I know that it's true'.

Plagiarism is no substitute for skill

To avoid plagiarism, writers need to understand the two closely related principles that source use should be transparent to the reader and serve a function in the text. In order to be able to implement these ideas, they must also possess a body of declarative knowledge and procedural competences about how sources are and are not used in academic writing, as well as more general writing skills. While listing all of those skills is properly the task of a writing manual, this chapter has sampled some of them.

In addition, writers also need to know about plagiarism. They need to know how it is defined, and what it looks like in practice, and they need to know that the consequences of plagiarism are serious. They also need to know that there are complexities in understanding what plagiarism is. However, the best prevention for plagiarism is to provide writers with a viable alternative. Ways of delivering the skills and knowledge needed to shape that alternative are the subject of the next chapter.

Activity

A survey of information given to students. Find the information about plagiarism and source use that is given to students at your university, and in your department or programme.

- Where is it? Is it part of the university rules, or study information on the library's website, or part of a study guide within a particular course?
- How is it delivered to students, and how are students made aware it exists?
- What sort of information does it provide about plagiarism? Does it offer a definition of plagiarism? Information about how to tell if a piece of writing is plagiarised?
- What sort of information does it offer about good source use? Does it describe referencing conventions? The reasons writers refer to sources? How to tell reliable sources from less reliable ones?

Questions for discussion or reflection

1 Can you remember having a difficult decision to make in your own writing about whether (or what sort of) a reference was needed? What caused the difficulty, and how did you resolve it?

2 When you read published work in your field, is it easy to infer how the writers have used sources? If not, why not?

3 At what point in their education do students in your department learn things such as how to paraphrase, how to introduce a quotation, how to prepare reference lists, etc.?

4 Does the transparency principle articulated in this chapter provide an explanation for the types of source use you do not want your students to use? Does it prevent any source use strategies you think they should be able to use?

5

How can teachers support student learning about source use?

Summary • Principles for a source-use curriculum • Approaches to teaching source use • Activity • Questions for discussion or reflection

Summary

This chapter describes how teachers can best support their students to gain the skills needed to avoid plagiarism. It describes how teachers can determine what their students need to learn about plagiarism and good source usage, and how an appropriate curriculum may be developed. Presenting students with declarative facts about source use is seen to be a limited approach and an argument is made for a process-based skills development approach. The framework for such an approach is discussed, including importance of explicit learning objectives for source-use skills. The use of text-matching ('plagiarism detection') software is explored. The chapter concludes with ten sample tasks provided for teachers which teach the key aspects of transparency, i.e. accurately reporting the content of a source, clearly signalling to the reader the identity of the source, choosing when to quote and when to paraphrase and how to paraphrase. The tasks are designed to be useful in a range of teaching contexts, and suggestions for adapting them to others are provided.

When you have finished this chapter you will understand how to plan and carry out instruction which will enable your students to develop the skills required to use sources well and make effective decisions about how to report material from a source and how to signal it to the reader.

Setting aside the risk of committing, or being suspected of, plagiarism, what do your students need to know about the role that reporting the earlier literature plays in constructing a successful new text? What are the most important of the 'assumptions and methods of scholarship' which Hunt refers to below? How much of that do they typically learn on their own, and how much do you teach them?

. . . by facing this challenge [Internet plagiarism] we will be forced to help our students learn what I believe to be the most important thing they can learn at university: just how the intellectual enterprise of scholarship and research really works. Traditionally, when we explain to students why plagiarism is bad and what their motives should be for properly citing and crediting their sources, we present them in terms of a model of how texts work in the process of sharing ideas and information which is profoundly different from how they actually work outside of classroom-based writing, and profoundly destructive to their understanding of the assumptions and methods of scholarship.

(Hunt, n.d.)

The previous chapter argued that the most effective cure for all patchwriting and some prototypical plagiarism is for students to learn the skills in using sources which will not only make their texts more effective but will offer a viable alternative to plagiarism as well. This chapter addresses the ways in which teachers can support that learning. The first section offers a generalised view of a learning environment which offers appropriate support, with reference to concepts related to teaching and learning which are especially relevant. The second part of the chapter consists of learning activities and tasks designed to help students master one or more skills related to learning to use sources.

Principles for a source-use curriculum

Any body of learning can best be delivered when there is progression across the degree programme, with consideration given to the abilities students already have when they begin it and their needs when they leave it. Taking progression into account involves asking, and finding the best pedagogical answers, to four questions:

1 What do students need to know (about source use, here) upon completion of their studies?

2 What do they already know about it when they arrive at university?
The answers to these questions provide a framework for answering the third:
3 What do they need to learn during their programme?
That then provides a starting point for identifying specific curricular implications:
4 When and how during their studies should the individual items included under (3) be introduced?

This idealised picture does not take into account several very real constraints and obstacles. First, it assumes that it is possible to define the knowledge and skills that students possess on arrival at university with a reasonable degree of accuracy, but in today's increasingly heterogeneous university classroom, this is not always the case (Chapters 7 and 9 take up aspects of this situation).

Second, it assumes that it is possible to plan a transition between learning at university and its applications in the workplace. However, with respect to writing skills, including but not limited to source use, this is very often not the case. Students often produce assessment genres – the essay, the critical response to a book, reflections on a learning platform – which bear little relation to the sorts of workplace writing they will do. Specifically, the ways in which many workplace genres use sources is at sharp odds with the conventions and principles of academic writing (Devitt, 1991; Shaw and Pecorari, 2013).

Finally, the luxury of large-scale planning is not one which belongs to most university teachers. Many are limited in the extent of their practical ability to change practice to the course or courses on which they teach, and even there constraints are likely to exist. So while an ideal approach to teaching source use would involve distributing the content discussed in Chapter 4 across the length of a degree programme, a more realistic approach for many teachers involves thinking about what their students need to learn within the framework of a specific part of a course, while maintaining the greatest awareness possible of what else students will learn, and need to learn, and where and when in their studies that will happen.

A precondition for good source use has already been seen to be a set of both knowledge and skills. For many teachers, imparting facts about this area is more comfortable than developing skills, because it makes it easier to present clear rules and unhedged assertions. However, the clear-cut declarative facts about source use which can be presented to students without excessive qualification are primarily those which relate to the mechanics of citation, and they are only a small part, and the least problematic part, of what must be learned.

The alternative, teaching skills as well as facts about source use, takes more planning and management on the part of the teacher. Learning a skill requires, in addition to input, opportunities to practice, feedback on performance, and fresh opportunities to practice in the light of the feedback. When teaching the basics of source use, it is tempting to avoid raising areas of uncertainty, particularly given that a failure to use sources appropriately may be interpreted as a matter of academic dishonesty. This raises the spectre that any acknowledgement that there are uncertainties to source use may be used as a defence against an allegation of wrongdoing. However, addressing the uncertainties is essential if students are to develop the skills of good source usage and proficient academic writing.

A useful concept in structuring these opportunities is constructive alignment (Biggs, 1996). Constructive alignment is the idea that there should be a thread of coherence linking learning objectives, learning activities and assessment. In other words, the planned outcome of a course should dictate the content of lectures and seminars, what students read, the formative tasks that scaffold their learning etc. At the end of this chain, the assessment activities should measure the attainment of the learning objectives, and the question a teacher brings to the assessment work is 'to what extent does this work demonstrate that the student has achieved the course objectives?'

Constructive alignment is a particularly useful model for shaping practices for teaching source use in that it requires that learning objectives be explicitly articulated. Objectives related to source use, or indeed any other aspect of academic writing or professional discourse, are only infrequently expressed as planned learning outcomes (although an exception exists for the language subjects, in which the ability to communicate in various forms is a primary focus of instruction and assessment). In most fields, though, assessment writing is a means to an end, the tool which exposes students' knowledge of the course content so that it can be assessed, rather than an objective in its own right.

While writing and source-use skills must necessarily take second place to other content in the majority of courses, there are problematic aspects to them being absent from the stated objectives altogether. There is not, for one thing, an absolute divide between language and content. For example, understanding terminology used in a particular subject requires an understanding of the underlying concepts, and an inability to use appropriate terminology can expose an insufficient understanding of the content. The ability to engage in professional discourse is one which will be necessary in the workplace, and is in fact an objective which many teachers say they pursue in their teaching, though in most cases it is an informal, unstated objective rather than a formally articulated one (Pecorari *et al.*, 2011). Importantly, objectives which are unstated rather than directly named are less likely to be planned for, and therefore much less likely to be reached.

Learning objectives

A pedagogy for promoting good source use and thereby eliminating plagiarism would then have as its starting point a set of learning objectives relating to what students should be able to do on completion of the assignment, the module, the degree course, etc. Chapter 3 described policies and procedures typically in place at universities, and students most certainly need to know them. Learning objectives related to plagiarism and what one may not do with sources can be summarised like this:

Students should be able to:

- articulate an understanding of what plagiarism is;
- identify it;
- demonstrate familiarity with the rules about plagiarism in place at their university;
- show an understanding of the procedures used at their university for detecting and responding to plagiarism;
- know where they can turn for more information.

The positive knowledge which will enable students to avoid plagiarism by using sources appropriately and effectively (as presented in Chapter 4) can be summarised like this. Students should be able to:

- identify reasons why sources are used in academic writing;
- find sources of information which are relevant to a particular writing topic;
- read and understand sources of a range of types;
- understand how sources have been used in texts which signal them transparently;
- paraphrase ideas from a source;
- summarise sources;
- make use of reporting language;
- integrate quotations, summaries and paraphrases smoothly into a new text;
- understand the relationship among sources and the new text;
- identify aspects of the writing topic which benefit from support from sources;
- report propositions from sources in a way which strengthens the new text;
- find out authorship and other bibliographical information from a source;
- signal to the reader which content is from a source and which is original to the writer;
- convey an accurate impression of what the source said;
- signal which sources have made a material contribution to the new work;
- signal whether the language in which content from a source is expressed is also from the source or an original reformulation.

Because these objectives relate to the performance of a skill – writing academic texts – achieving them requires scaffolded opportunities for practice with feedback. Although the specifics of what this entails will differ from one teaching context to another, several central ideas can serve to structure such an approach.

Learning activities

One key idea is that there is a logical progression in the learning of source-use skills. Not only are there a great many subskills which are part of learning to write from sources, some of them build upon others. For instance, the ability to paraphrase successfully is dependent on the ability to read a source actively and critically and understand its content thoroughly enough to offer an independent retelling of it. In order to be able to relate ideas from different sources to each other, the writer must have been able to find a range of sources on the same topic. This observation has two important implications for classroom practice. One is that it can be useful to teach the subskills of citation separately, before addressing them in the context of a large writing assignment. The exercises in the second half of this chapter are one way of doing this. The second implication is that the order in which subskills should be presented should be determined by conscious decision, in the light of the desired outcomes (what students must learn by the end of their degree course, or in ability to complete a piece of assessed work, etc.) and bearing in mind what skills they (are likely to) possess already.

When source use is practiced as part of a larger writing assignment, care in crafting the assignment is needed. A task which offers students a foothold so that they can develop a thesis and genuinely have something to say will make it easier for them to place that message as the centrepiece of the writing assignment and use sources to support it. A vague or uninspiring writing task about which writers have little they want to communicate is an invitation to introducing reference after reference to sources to fill space. It is possible to avoid plagiarism in such an assignment, but it is not possible to use sources effectively, when a clear sense of the text's purpose, and the sources' intended effect, is lacking.

The terms of the assignment are also important in shaping good preconditions for diagnosing problems when they arise. The responsibility of transparency was shown in the previous chapter to be important precisely because many aspects of source use are ordinarily invisible to the reader. The reason a great deal of textual plagiarism is undetected is because there is nothing in the text to signal a problem, to raise warning flags. Yet the absence of comments about source use will be taken by students to mean that they are doing the right things. For feedback to be effective, then, it must either identify problems or make a clear statement that there are none.

For this to happen, teachers must read actively in the awareness that there may be problems and try to spot them, and not assume that all problems will make themselves visible. Many teachers are, of course, skilled at recognising signs that there may be a problem. A familiarity with the student's previous performance on writing assignments or in class discussions can help. In addition, patchwriting often leaves visible traces at the seams where the source's language is stitched together with the student's and this style shift can alert teachers to a problem. However, giving good feedback requires a greater accuracy in identifying problems than even the most experienced teacher can be expected to provide, relying only on instinct.

One way of achieving the preconditions for identifying problems is to create writing assignments which involve the students drawing upon a small selection of sources, possibly just one, with which the teacher is familiar. Such an assignment must be specific and structured in such a way that students, in their responses, will have a communicative purpose. A 'purposeless' assignment, such as summarising a book or an article, is an invitation to patchwriting. (Task 10 at the end of this chapter gives an example of a successful assignment.)

Another approach is to use a writing conference or time in class to invite students to show each other and you how they have used their sources. They should bring their sources, to make side-by-side comparisons possible and describe how they have used sources (e.g., by paraphrasing or quoting), which sources they have used and why, and what purposes each reference to sources serves in their text. This creates a setting in which questions about uncertainties are likely to be asked and problems stand a good chance of being exposed.

Text-matching software can be used to identify problems before they reach final draft stage. Chapter 3 gave a number of caveats relating to the use of these products, and they apply to their use for formative assessment as well as summative. There are risks of false negatives as well as false positives, and the additional risk that students may take away the message that good source use can be equated with a number of a text-matching reports. When close similarities with a source are identified, a student approach to addressing them is often to make extensive superficial changes: substituting more synonyms, changing more active verbs to passive, etc., and while these changes do indeed have the effect of lowering the proportion of their work identified as copied, they amount to a sort of thorough-going patchwriting, not good writing from sources.

A risk of using text-matching software as a training aid is thus that it can confirm patchwriting strategies rather than discouraging them. In addition, students who are attempting, or are likely to attempt to cheat learn from practice how to produce texts which will not reveal an awkward degree of similarity to sources. In other words, they can learn to game the system. If products like these are used as part of the writing process, it is essential that these issues be problematised. Rather than presenting the results of a comparison as if they provided an answer on which further work can be based, results can serve as the basis of a classroom discussion in which students are made aware of the limitations of such a report, and thus come to a more mature understanding of source use in academic writing.

Any sort of formative feedback presupposes a multi-draft writing process in which students will be given a chance to revise, and this has many concomitant positive effects. One of these is that it models an effective way to write: revision is just as important in good writing as the initial drafting. Another is that it creates a situation in which students' decisions about revision can be made with reference to the central thesis and the goals they want the text to accomplish. They can be urged make their decisions about revision not in the absolute ('is it better to use this word or that?') but in terms of which alternative will be most helpful in making readers understand what the writer wants them to.

A multi-draft process may also create a space for teachers to respond pedagogically to textual plagiarism which they would not otherwise have. At some institutions, teachers are required to report suspected plagiarism to some authority. This situation can force an uncomfortable decision on them: to report or ignore. By contrast, early drafts can be considered exercises rather than part of the formal assessment, and therefore can be a possible terrain in which the rules do not apply.

Finally creating a training space for source use is only fully effective if the teacher is prepared for the reality that some source use will be inappropriate, and some of that will constitute textual plagiarism. By virtue of the fact that plagiarism is associated with cheating and other acts of academic dishonesty, some teachers have a strong emotional reaction to it when they identify it, understanding it to be indicative of a breakdown of trust, or a sort of betrayal. An implication of source use being a skill is that some students will get it wrong, even after they have been told, possibly repeatedly. A dispassionate reaction to textual plagiarism which puts the student's achievement of the learning objectives in the centre is the one which offers the best opportunity for success.

Assessment

Forms of assessment vary, naturally, from course to course, and may or may not be within the control of the teacher to change. In contexts where formative assessment is used, writing tasks as discussed in the preceding section may be both learning activities and the assessment for the course. Two additional ideas relate exclusively to the written work as assessment, and, given that the constructive alignment model shows assessment to be a development of learning objectives, both are connected to objectives.

The first concerns the role of intention. Intention is both central in understanding whether an instance of problematic source use should be seen as evidence that the student has more to learn, or evidence that the student is attempting to cheat. At the same time, guilty intent is difficult both to be certain about and to prove. A constructive alignment framework for teaching about source use can to some extent alleviate this difficulty. If aspects of source use are part of the learning objectives, then they must also be part of the assessment criteria. If assessment criteria include items such as demonstrating the ability to formulate ideas from a source in independent wordings, signal the content which comes from a source transparently, and use references to sources to support an original thesis or argument which is of the student's own making, then both patchwriting and prototypical plagiarism are signs that the student has not attained the learning objectives. This means that, regardless of whether deceptive plagiarism attracts a punishment, it will not trigger a reward in the form of a grade.

It is very important to distinguish this from the use of a lowered grade as a form of punishment. A lowered grade as a response to deceptive plagiarism – a common practice – sends two signals: that a rule was violated, but the violation was relatively trivial (in that lowered grades are at the small end of the continuum of punishments for plagiarism which range up to suspension or even expulsion, and, after the fact, the withdrawal of a degree). That must be done within an institutional regulatory framework which specifies that grades can be used as a form of punishment (and the soundness of that as a pedagogical method can be debated). However, if signalling source use transparently is part of the learning objectives for a course, then there is a basis for saying that a student who has done it partially, but not entirely successfully can receive a grade for the work, but not the highest one.

A further, closely related issue is to do with student expectations. Developing source-use skills (along with other sorts of academic writing skills) is, to repeat a point made earlier, more often an implicit and unstated objective than an explicit one. The institutional implications of this will be addressed in Chapter 6. In the classroom, it is important that teachers make all objectives explicit. Making students aware that they will be expected to develop good source-use skills greatly increases the likelihood that they will be able to meet those expectations.

Approaches to teaching source use

The previous section provided a principled description of an effective way to plan for, deliver and assess instruction in using sources effectively, in order to empower students to avoid plagiarism. This section offers specific tasks and assignments which can be used to teach aspects of source-use skills. These may need to be adapted for some teaching contexts, and suggestions are given for how this may be done. One alternative, which is highlighted in some tasks but can be exploited more broadly, is to select texts from your subject area to analyse with students. Both good examples of polished, published writing and more and less successful student assessment work can be used to show students how sources are used, to better and less good effect, in the subject area.

These tasks also serve as illustrations of the ways in which the subskills of source use can be worked with, and may offer ideas for further activities. Tasks 1–3 deal primarily with aspects of transparent reporting of source content, tasks 4–6 with signalling the identity of the source, and tasks 7–9 with transparency of language. Task 10 is a description of a writing assignment which gives the opportunity to practice a range of source-use skills.

There is a sequential nature to the tasks, so that within each group, the first task lays a foundation for the others. Task 1, for example, asks the student to read and derive information while task 3 involves active choices about wording for reporting source content.

Task 1. Extracting content from a source with accuracy

Objective: The purpose of this exercise is to raise awareness of the need to read actively and critically. It aims to underscore the fundamental importance of reading as a learning activity by highlighting the ways that components of the reading process, such as extracting main ideas and relating specific facts to each other, lead to a better understanding of the text.

Procedures: Distribute this extract from an undergraduate textbook in psychology in advance of a class meeting, and ask students to read it and bring it to class. Ask them to answer the questions below, one at a time. After each question, ask some people to share their answers and discuss what the components of a good answer would be.

> For our discussion in this chapter, we will define aggression as physical or verbal behavior intended to cause harm. This definition excludes unintentional harm such as auto accidents or sidewalk collisions; it also excludes actions that may involve pain as an unavoidable side effect of helping someone, such as dental treatments or – in the extreme – assisted suicide. It includes kicks and slaps, threats and insults, even gossip or snide 'digs'; and decisions, during experiments, about how much to hurt someone, such as how much electric shock to impose. It also includes destroying property, lying, and other behavior whose goal is to hurt.
>
> The definition covers two distinct types of aggression. Animals exhibit social aggression, characterized by displays of rage; and silent aggression, as when a predator stalks its prey. Social and silent aggression involve separate brain regions. In humans, psychologists label the two types 'hostile' and 'instrumental' aggression. Hostile aggression springs from anger; its goal is to injure. Instrumental aggression aims to injure, too – but only as a means to some other end.

Questions

(a) What is the overall purpose of these paragraphs? Answer in not more than one sentence.
(b) What does the second paragraph add to the first one?
(c) What does the author see as the key elements in this definition of aggression? How do you know?
(d) Are there other ways to define aggression? How do you know?

Note on answers

(a) The purpose of the two paragraphs is to provide a definition of aggression. The framing of this question is important because it puts an emphasis on the writer's objectives and encourages students to understand the writer's task as relating content *for a purpose.*

(b) It articulates two subcategories of aggression and shows how they each meet the criteria of the broad definition but are distinct from each other. Some students may provide more general answers such as 'it adds more detail'. The purpose of this question is to encourage students to relate ideas in their sources to each other, so they should be urged to develop such general statements until that happens.

(c) The most obvious answer is that the author sees 'harm' and 'intention' as the key ingredients. Evidence for this conclusion comes from the fact that both those components are present in the first, most general definition; both are present as well in the definitions of the subcategories of aggression ('its goal is to injure'; 'aims to injure'); and the acts which are excluded from this definition are ones in which the harm is accidental or unintentional. It is important to encourage students to provide evidence from the text for their conclusions, to underline the idea that a close reading can produce a better understanding of the text.

(d) The qualification at the beginning 'for our discussion in this chapter' suggests that there are other ways aggression could be defined. Here too, it is important that students find this textual evidence for their answers, to demonstrate that they can draw fact-based conclusions from what they read.

Task 2. Relating content accurately

Objective: To encourage students to think critically about whether a paraphrase of a source is an accurate retelling or a distortion.

Procedures: Distribute the following examples of student writing which includes a reference to a source. Do these students convey the content of their sources transparently? That is, would a reader who saw only the student's work, and not the source, form the correct view of how the writers had used their sources? Why or why not? Follow up with an example from your field, giving the students both the report of a source and an extract from the original. The discussion may turn up criticisms of the paraphrases which you think are unfounded, as well as criticisms that are. There may be questions which are difficult to resolve, but the process of thinking critically about whether two expressions of the same idea are equivalent will be beneficial.

Student

Watkins says that the main contribution of pastoral care may be that it brings 'attention to the personal and interpersonal dimensions and to give a pupil-centred focus' (1985: 179).

Source (Watkins, 1985: 179)

The broad ambition of pastoral care is to help pupils benefit more extensively from their school experience. But this is surely the broad aim of any school, so is it worth saying? Yes, if we go on to say that the more specific contribution of pastoral care is to bring attention to the personal and interpersonal dimensions, and to give a pupil-centred focus.

Student

'Teachers are part of a very complicated social system . . . which determines at times, his or her view of self and of the system and of the teaching techniques' (Sarason, p. 32).

Source (Sarason, p. 32)

First, the university critic is part of a very complicated social system that, in diverse ways, determines his or her view of self and that system.

Note on answers: A significant difference between the first student's report and the source is that the source speaks of the 'more specific contribution' of pastoral care, while the student says it is the 'main contribution'. Some students may feel that this is justified because this writer has been more cautious in her claim about the contribution: while the source says that a 'more specific contribution . . . **is** . . .', the writer says it '**may be**'. However, this hedging arguably introduces greater inaccuracy, rather than mitigating the first. The author of the source makes a direct claim, while the report of the source makes him appear to be more hesitant than he was (albeit about a different proposition).

The second student has taken a claim from the source but applied it to a different concept. What the source says about the 'university critic' appears in the student's work to apply to teachers. While the claim may be true and may even be one with which the author of the source would agree, it gives a misleading impression of what the source actually said.

Task 3. Signalling orientations to content

Objectives: An element in reporting the propositional content from a source is indicating the way that the source author positions him – or herself in relation to it. The writer's own evaluation of the content can be visible in the report of the source, or withheld. The purpose of this activity is to raise awareness of the way that language choices when reporting content from sources can shape the way the content will be received by the reader.

Procedures: Distribute to students the following sentence and the verbs which appear below it. Ask them to fill in the blank with each of the reporting verbs in turn, and discuss how the impact of the sentence changes as a result. Specific questions to consider are

(1) Which versions of the sentence make the author (Gorgonzola) appear to agree, disagree, or remain neutral about the idea (i.e., that the moon is made of green cheese)? Do some of them convey their meaning more strongly than others?
(2) Which versions make the writer of this sentence appear to agree with Gorgonzola, disagree, or remain neutral?

Gorgonzola _____ that the moon is made of green cheese.
acknowledges
argues
asserts
believes
concludes
demonstrates
denies
hypothesises
posits
states
suggests

Note on answers: The author's commitment to the idea: *denies* indicates that Gorgonzola disagrees with this idea; the others describe some kind of agreement. Of these, *hypothesises, posits* and *suggests* imply a relatively weaker commitment on Gorgonzola's part toward the idea. By hypothesising, for example, Gorgonzola indicates that the idea is something which can be tested and may be disproved. The writer's evaluation of the idea: *Acknowledges* and *demonstrates* indicate that the writer believes Gorgonzola is right. The others reveal little about what the writer thinks. Note that this is true even of *denies,* which casts Gorgonzola in opposition to the idea, but does not say whether the writer thinks that opposition is founded.

Alternative: If this particular selection of reporting verbs is not typical of those in your field, take a few paragraphs from the introduction to a research article in your field, remove the reporting verbs, and use the resulting sentences and list of verbs to do this exercise. Another alternative still is to distribute a complete text and ask students to find the reporting verbs and discuss differences in their meanings, as well as the reasons the author may have chosen the forms he or she did.

Task 4. Identifying the author of a work

Objective: To make students aware of the variety of forms of publication, enabling them to understand who should be credited as the originator of a work, and what possible sources of information are available.

Procedures: Have students work in groups of 3–6. Provide each group with an example of three or four types of publications which are commonly referred to as sources of information in your discipline, for example, an academic journal, a monograph, a technical report, an anthology. Ask students to discuss similarities and differences among the works and then to say, for each one, who wrote it. Follow up by asking why the differences they identified exist; that is, why do there need to be different forms of publication?

Note on answers: Answers will of course vary, but there are several important points which need to come out of students' exploration of these works. One is that not all publications are the work of a single author; a monograph may be, although it may have multiple authors, while an issue of a research journal contains multiple articles, each of which may have one author or several. The answer to the question 'who wrote it' will therefore be 'many people'. Technical reports, on the other hand, may not identify an author at all. The discussion of similarities and differences among the publications should lead to an answer to the question about why there are different sorts of publications: periodicals offer a relatively fast way to disseminate new research findings, anthologies or edited collections allow individual works to be published together with other, thematically linked papers which inform them. Conclude by noting that searching key words in the library catalogue will identify books on a topic but not journal articles, and recommend a course on information searching at the university library.

Task 5. Gathering and reporting bibliographic information

Objectives: This task builds on the previous one and teaches finding and presenting bibliographic details.

Procedures: Use the same selection of texts as for the previous task, and a description of the correct formatting for a reference list entry for each one, according to a set of style conventions frequently used in your field. Teach the format for one type of source and ask students to practice by writing a reference list entry for one of the works in front of them. Then move on to another type of source.

Note on answers: Answers will naturally vary, but some information is often hard for inexperienced academic readers to find initially, and may prompt questions. For example, the date of publication typically appears prominently in a research article, but in a book it may appear only as the copyright date on the colophon (behind the title page). The editors of an anthology are specified in reference-list entries but the editors of a journal are not. Point out that the sort of information included in an entry is the information a reader would need to find the source.

Alternative: Following up by contrasting with a *different* set of conventions (e.g. MLA and APA) has the advantage of underscoring the idea that referencing conventions are a largely arbitrary set of rules which exist to allow the higher-order function of signalling source use to be carried out consistently within a publication.

Task 6. Relationships among sources

Objectives: The collection of sources referred to in a literature review can be partially or entirely in agreement with each other, in opposition to each other, or pursuing different aspects of the same problem. These relationships are often clearer to experienced writers in the area than they are to students. The purpose of this activity is to illustrate the relationships among sources by looking at one such relationship, self-citation.

Procedures: Select the title page and reference lists from one or more publications in your subject area. Ask students to work in pairs to identify how often the author has cited him- or herself. If any of those citations are co-authored, ask the students then to find how many other times the co-authors are cited.

Note on answers: This activity works best if the publications selected are those which have some self-citation, but to a degree which is normal, rather than excessive, in the field. If alphabetically ordered reference lists are used, this task will take less time than if numbered end references are used, and with the former systems the fact of self-citation will also be more evident in the body of the text itself.

Task 7. Choosing to quote or paraphrase

Objective: To make students aware of the frequency with which quotation and paraphrase are used in their subject area, and of some of the factors which guide that decision.

Procedures: Supply students with a text which you consider to be a good example of source use in your discipline. Ask students to identify quotations and paraphrases, and to discuss in small groups why the author chooses to introduce an idea from the source in that form.

Note on answers: Draw students' attention to the fact that paraphrases are identified by eliminating ideas which are attributed to a source but which are not signalled as quotation. Although it is not possible to answer the question of the author's choices definitively, there is a tendency to quote only when a paraphrase will not do, for example, if an idea is a very sensitive one and subject to distortion, or when not only the idea but the form in which it is expressed is important to conveying the idea, or when it is expressed in a succinct way which communicates the message clearly. In most areas in the humanities and social sciences quotation is used in a minority of cases, but a significant minority. In a few fields, such as comparative literature, the form of expression has particular importance and quotation is the dominant form. In the natural sciences and engineering quotation is used exceedingly rarely. If you teach one of these fields, this activity is useful only in abbreviated form for the purpose of illustrating the rarity of quotation.

Task 8. Producing quotations and paraphrases

Objectives: To illustrate that quotation and paraphrase serve partially distinct purposes; to offer practice integrating both forms into a larger text.

Procedures: Provide students with a short excerpt from two or three of the sources referred to in the text used in task 7. Then ask them to turn a quotation into a paraphrase, and a paraphrase into a quotation. Have them discuss the decisions which had to be made in the process. Was it difficult to find a good candidate for a quotation? How did they decide where to start and stop the quotation? Was anything of value lost in turning a quotation into a paraphrase?

Notes on answers: Allow ample time for this activity as it will give rise to a number of procedural questions which will need answering. Draw these out and present the answers to the class as a whole. Use this occasion to check that the paraphrasing process involves independent rewording of an idea, not just substituting key words (see also the next task). Most students will experience greater difficulty integrating the quotation into the text than the paraphrase, since the language of the quotation must be retained, and therefore the surrounding text must be shaped to accommodate it. If your students have a tendency to overuse quotation, raise this point to illustrate that quotation is not necessarily an easier rhetorical task than paraphrase.

Task 9. A paraphrase process

Objectives: To illustrate that paraphrase builds on a confident understanding of the source, and the form a paraphrase takes will depend on the purpose which the reference to the source serves in the new text.

Procedures: Ask students to read a research article which you assign before class. It should be an exemplar of clear and concise writing in your field. In class ask them the following questions, one by one, and ask them to write a single sentence in response to each question. They should not look at the article while answering the questions.

(a) What question did the researcher set out to answer?
(b) How did the researcher investigate that question?
(c) What did the researcher find out in answer to the question?
(d) What does that finding mean? That is, what implications does it have?

After students have written their one-sentence answers to these questions, ask them to put the sentences away and take out the article, and ask them to check whether the answers they gave were the best possible ones. After a suitable interval, ask them to put away the articles and take out the one-sentence answers and offer them a chance to revise them. Then ask some students to share their responses, and put one or more good answers on the board.

Notes on answers: By requiring students to write without direct reference to the source, this task illustrates that the task of paraphrasing is one of explaining what the writer knows about the source rather than making minor changes to the source. Asking for a one-sentence response requires students to distil the main ideas out of each of the four areas canonically addressed in research articles: introduction, methods, results and discussion.

Alternative: If a research article will be too difficult for your students, or if it does not fit into the format of the class for some reason, this basic activity – asking students to answer questions about content without reference to the source – can be done successfully with other sorts of texts, but most easily with texts which exemplify a well defined genre whose form can be used to structure the activity.

Task 10. Integrating source-use skills

Objectives: To develop students' abilities to draw on a variety of source-use skills to support a claim within a longer text.

Procedures: Students are asked to read a book and write an assignment responding to a particular aspect of it. The assignment must be specific and involve the student developing, and putting forward, an argument or thesis. For example, students can read Bill Bryson's book *Down Under*, and write about the three key words which Bryson would agree capture the nature of Australia, supplying evidence for the claim from the book. (A variation of this assignment can work well with any book-length text which has a relatively clear thesis, is written at a level that students can understand, and ideally has some relationship to the course content. The question in the prompt must, naturally, be tailored to fit the book.) Students should submit a first draft and receive feedback on it, including specifically how appropriately and effectively they refer to the source, and an opportunity to revise based on feedback.

Notes on answers: Because Bryson does not identify three key words in the book, the task requires students to identify overarching themes in the book, and develop claims which they can then support with textual evidence. This puts the references to the source in a supporting position in relation to the larger text. Because the book and the student assignment are on different if related topics (Bryson's book is about Australia, while the assignment is about the book) it is very difficult to incorporate patchwritten chunks, provided the student focuses on the topic and answers the prompt, and writes about Bryson's view of Australia, rather than getting sidetracked with a thesis about *his or her own* perceptions of Australia. (This activity was developed by Karin Molander Danielsson, who has generously allowed it to be used here.)

Activity

A case study of an assessment activity. Select a course at your institution which is not one on which you teach, and which has a form of assessment which requires students to read and refer to other sources.

- What expectations do teachers on this course have about how students should use sources? Interview one or more teachers to find out.
- What instruction are students on this course given about how they should use sources in this assignment? Gather any written documentation they are given, and ask the teacher(s) if they tell students things that are not included in the written instructions.
- What are students told about plagiarism? Is there anything that they are expected to know about writing from sources which is *not* taught in this course? If so, where is it taught (e.g., was it part of an earlier course?).
- Are there formal assessment criteria for this assignment? If so, do they deal with source use?

Questions for discussion or reflection

1 What source-use skills, and other writing skills generally, do students need to produce the assessment tasks you commonly work with?
2 Which of those skills do they know when they reach your classroom, and which do they still need to learn?
3 Which of the skills for writing from sources that students must demonstrate in order to finish a degree at your institution, will be directly useful later in the workplace? Which will have indirect, transferable outcomes?

6

What support can institutions offer?

Summary

Given the costs, time and reputational damage that can be caused by plagiarism and the disputes often attendant on it, academic institutions need to take all reasonable steps to avoid them. The policies, regulations and definitions not only need to enable plagiarism to be detected and the appropriate responses applied, they also need to require that sources are used appropriately so that plagiarism, and the unfortunate consequences for the university, the teacher and the student, are avoided.

Essential to achieving this are good policies. Policies need to be clear about where the responsibilities lie for making students aware of what plagiarism is and for teaching good source use. The institution must take responsibility for seeing that appropriate materials and instruction are available and delivered at the most effective points in the curriculum. A further area of institutional responsibility is ensuring that teachers have the required skills and training to help their students with these issues (particularly in regard to interpreting the output of text matching tools). Resources and support are needed by both students and teachers. Policies and practices must provide for effective handling of both prototypical plagiarism and patchwriting. While penalties for intentional plagiarism are required, where deception is not involved, the use of penalties is counterproductive. Alternative remedies are therefore needed.

After having read this chapter you will be able to be able to assess and contribute to the improvement of your institution's policies on plagiarism and the responses to it for the benefit of the university, the teachers and the students.

What expectations does your institution place on teachers in terms of preventing, detecting and responding to plagiarism? What support does it give them in doing those things? Specifically, does it do the things Sutherland-Smith calls for below? If not, what are the obstacles? Does your institution go further and provide forms of support not named below?

Universities also charge academic staff and students with the responsibility for appropriate citation practice education. This raises questions about the university's responsibilities in a number of ways. Universities must provide sufficient training for staff (including casual and part-time academic staff involved in teaching and assessment), particularly where anti-plagiarism software programs are used. It is not sufficient for the institution to merely place the additional workload of teaching students about citation and attribution concepts and mechanics without attention to the need for staff professional development in this area and also the additional time taken to fulfil such requirements.

(Sutherland-Smith, 2010: 9)

This book so far has addressed teachers (and people in related roles, such as consultants working in writing centres and study skills workshops), who are at the front line of meeting student concerns about source use and plagiarism. The present chapter discusses the role academic institutions can play in preventing plagiarism and promoting good source use, and as a result, it speaks primarily to administrators and other staff who have the ability and responsibility to shape policy and standards for practice and steer the allocation of resources.

If you are reading this chapter as an educational administrator, you have a problem with plagiarism. You have a problem because academic institutions want to eliminate plagiarism, and yet it happens at your university, and you know it happens more often than it is detected. You have a public image problem, because an increase in reported cases of plagiarism can make your student body appear dishonest, and a decrease can make your staff look soft on plagiarism. You have a financial problem because convening disciplinary boards and buying in 'plagiarism-detection' software is expensive, in addition to the invisible cost of the hours staff spend on detecting and reporting cases, which is time they cannot spend teaching. You also have a problem because staff experience stress when they have to initiate formal procedures against a student, and feel exposed and undervalued if they believe the wrong outcome is attained. You have a problem because some students plagiarise deliberately and get away with it, and others, who do not intend to cheat are bewildered and frustrated to be punished for what they did not know was wrong, and a third group are angry because they know some students plagiarise and are not caught. Tuition fees and the commodification of higher education means that students who think they have been treated unfairly are increasingly likely to vote with their feet and study somewhere else, or even sue their universities, and that is a problem too.

If the administrative problems caused by plagiarism are easy to set forth, the solutions are less so. This is in part because there is no magic bullet to cure plagiarism. It occurs at the intersection of a number of complex educational phenomena. Responding to plagiarism involves a constellation of structural, economic and legal issues which vary from country to country, and to some extent from institution to institution. The latitude which universities have to decide their own policies and procedures, the forms of assessment which are in use and the proclivity of students to go to law if they feel unfairly handled are all examples of the factors which must shape an institutional response to plagiarism.

The solution, then, must be tailored to the individual institution. The purpose of this chapter is to describe the areas in which institutional action can be effective in eliminating plagiarism and promoting effective source use, and to outline key elements of good practice. Chapter 1 described two sharply distinct forms of plagiarism which, by virtue of having different causes, demand different responses. This chapter addresses institutional responses first to prototypical plagiarism, and then to patchwriting.

Managing prototypical plagiarism

Chapter 3 described the usual response to plagiarism as a quasi-judicial one: rules are made, and made public; more or less formal detection methods are put in place; and when cases of plagiarism are suspected, there follows a process of deciding whether or not the suspicions are founded, and if so, penalties are decided. This mechanism is reasonably well suited to dealing with prototypical plagiarism, plagiarism which is the result of a student's deliberate effort to gain advantage by concealing the ways sources have been used. Opportunities for improving the response to plagiarism lie in refining the way each of these steps is carried out.

Policy and regulation

Successful policies, including the definitions of plagiarism within them, have two key characteristics. First, they need to reflect the institution's shared understanding of plagiarism. There are, for example, differences across academic subject areas in how sources are appropriately used, and therefore possible differences in how plagiarism is understood (see Chapter 8). If policy describes an act which some staff do not understand to be wrongdoing, the risk is that they will not enforce the policy. Good practice in the area of policy therefore includes seeing that it is the result of broad consensus following a serious consultation process so that the resulting rules and definitions are ones with which staff will engage.

A second characteristic of good policy is that it be specific enough to leave staff confident that they know how to apply it. A characteristic of many policies seen in Chapter 1 is that they define plagiarism in such general terms that staff experience difficulty knowing whether specific instances of student work should be regarded as plagiarism. While applying any rule to a given case requires an act of judgement, effective policy should provide staff with good tools for that judgement.

Spreading the word

The most desirable outcome for a policy on plagiarism is that it is so effective in providing both a carrot and a stick, telling students what they will gain by not plagiarising and what they will lose if they do, that students never consider plagiarism. One precondition for this is the clarity and specificity of rules and definitions mentioned above. If staff have difficulty understanding whether student work is plagiarised (and they do), it cannot be easier for students. In addition, the information needs to reach them in a form which they will notice, read, and engage with.

Detection

Detecting deceptive plagiarism is important, not only so that students do not receive academic awards based on efforts that were not their own, but so that the work of honest students is not devalued. Increasingly universities purchase subscriptions to text-matching ('plagiarism-detection') services in the hope that routinely scanning student work will result in more consistent responses. It is important to understand the limitations on what these services can do and the need for staff training if they are used. Chapter 3 details the pros and cons of text-matching services and describes other methods as alternatives or complements.

Mechanisms

It is customary in the English-speaking world and in many other countries for procedures to require some or all cases of suspected plagiarism to be referred to a disciplinary panel, an academic integrity officer, or some other individual or body who is not the teacher. A very sound reason for such procedures is to avoid a situation in which the teacher is simultaneously prosecutor, judge and jury. However, the success of a set of procedures which require the teacher to refer the case elsewhere depends on a number of elements which are often either absent or perceived by staff as absent.

First, the procedures should be known to all staff and as easy as possible to comply with. Since many teachers, fortunately, encounter plagiarism only infrequently, they may not know how to start the process. A clear step-by-step description of the process needs to be available where staff can find it easily and information to the effect that there are procedures needs to go out regularly, insuring that new and temporary staff are kept informed. Staff frequently perceive the reporting process as being time-consuming (Day, 2008; Sutherland-Smith, 2010), and as requiring 'extra time'. This may or may not match the reality from an administrative perspective; for example, the teacher time allocated to any given course may be intended to cover eventualities such as the need to report a case of plagiarism. However, if the procedures are perceived as putting an unrealistic burden on staff, they may not always be followed.

Second, the process should leave staff feeling that their efforts in following it are appreciated. However, too often this is not the case. Particularly when the accusation of plagiarism is not upheld, staff report feeling undermined and under attack. Not infrequently there is direct or implied criticism of the staff member; for example, if the accusation could not be upheld because the required warnings or information about plagiarism had not been supplied at the beginning of the course. However, such criticism should be delivered as tactfully as any formative feedback, for the purpose of ensuring improved performance in the future. Again, a process which is perceived to have a negative backlash against the member of staff who initiates it risks not being followed.

Finally, it is at the point of starting a disciplinary process that prototypical plagiarism and patchwriting merge in potentially risky ways. Frequently the possible outcomes of formal proceedings are binary: the student is either found guilty or is not. However, this results in an inappropriate outcome for many students produce work which is overly reliant on its sources in inappropriate ways but which is not motivated by intentional deception. Responding to such work is the subject of the next section, but it should be noted here that a safety valve should exist in the system for such writers in one or both of two places: at the point when a decision is made to make a formal report of possible plagiarism, and at the point when a decision is made.

Penalties

Penalties for plagiarism vary greatly across institutions and according to the perceived seriousness of the offence, and extend from a warning to a lowered grade at the small end of the spectrum, to suspension or expulsion or the revocation of a degree at the serious end. Particularly in the UK, a current effort is aimed at establishing 'penalty tariffs', sliding scales for certain predefined categories of plagiarism intended to make punishment fit the crime, and to create greater consistency in the process.

While this is a laudable objective, there are two potential pitfalls for institutions adopting a tariff system. The first is that to be implemented consistently, there must be a consistent view among all regulators as to what constitutes minor and serious plagiarism, and that must be grounded in broad consensus among the institution's staff. However, university teachers are inconsistent in deciding how to regard potential plagiarism (Pecorari and Shaw, 2012; Roig, 2001; Sutherland-Smith, 2008). Developing a tariff system which can successfully be applied is therefore not an easy matter.

A second essential point is, again, that there needs to be a response to plagiarism which is not deceptive in nature. Possible responses are suggested below, but an essential point is that there be an alternative which is not punitive in nature. Responding to unintentional plagiarism with any punishment, however mild, is akin to treating a cold with surgery. Minor surgery may cause the patient less discomfort than major, but it is no more appropriate a response.

Managing patchwriting

Patchwriting was defined in Chapter 1 as a form of textual plagiarism which is *not* caused by the intention to cheat. There is a lot of patchwriting (Pecorari, 2003; Howard, Serviss and Rodrigue, 2010), and preventing and responding to it effectively require fundamentally different measures than those which address prototypical plagiarism.

The very best prevention for patchwriting is good teaching, and Chapter 5 described ways in which teachers can work with this issue. The role of the larger institution in supporting them is twofold: providing resources and coordinating. Teaching students not to misuse sources means teaching them how to write effective academic texts which use sources appropriately. However, many teachers perceive that they are not adequately resourced to teach academic writing. They see teaching about writing as being in competition for time in their courses with the main content of their disciplines, and they have to prioritise the latter. They may also feel that while they are good at writing up their own research, teaching writing requires a skill set they do not have. An effective institutional response consists both of providing the resources so that students from all subjects can learn important writing skills, and in professional development efforts which help teachers across the curriculum learn to be skilled teachers of writing in their fields.

Such efforts can be complemented by obligatory or mandatory writing courses, writing centres, study support etc. These are more common at some institutions than others, and exist in a range of forms with different levels of resourcing but a general principle is that any writing support is better than none at all. However, writing skills develop slowly and after practice, and a single course, or even a series of writing courses cannot be expected to do away with students' need for writing support. It is therefore important that all staff who use writing for assessment purposes be equipped, both in time resources and skills, to guide students through the process of understanding and meeting expectations about how they will use sources.

Another important domain for institutional support is coordination. The skills students need to use sources effectively and appropriately – and thereby avoid plagiarism – develop incrementally, and to some extent according to a logical progression, as discussed in Chapter 5. As a result the expectations that can reasonably be placed on student performance and the input that is needed to ensure good preconditions for success depend on what input and opportunities for practice the student has had to date, and best planning for teaching source use takes into account the student's progression across the entire course of study. This is not a level of planning, though, which individual teachers can all engage in, or even be aware of. Nor can they reinvent the wheel and teach students everything they need to know about writing from sources each term. Regardless of where and when the provision of teaching about source use happens across the curriculum, then an important role for the institution, then, is to see to it that it *does* happen; that longsighted planning is in place to ensure that all students across all subjects have the opportunity to learn the things they need to complete their assessment writing tasks.

Unifying the management of textual plagiarism

The two sections above dealt with the two forms of textual plagiarism, prototypical plagiarism and patchwriting, separately, because they are very different acts and deserve different responses. The first, a form of cheating, requires sanctions; the second requires a pedagogical response. However, two opportunities for institutional response are equally effective against both.

The teacher is the key actor in preventing and responding to plagiarism of both sorts, and must perform a wide range of functions: informing students about rules and policies, providing instruction in source-use skills, detecting textual plagiarism, deciding what response to it is most appropriate, etc. A useful support function for teachers is a point of consultation, a confidential advisor who can help them decide whether a particular case of plagiarism is deceptive or not, advise on designing assignments which encourage an original response, etc. Such a resource could also support teachers who report cases of plagiarism in the process so that it becomes a less negative experience.

Another valuable institutional function is shaping admissions procedures. The need exists to coordinate instruction in source use and writing to see to it that all students are equipped for their writing tasks because in many contexts systematic instruction in subject-based writing is not common. Source-use skills along with other writing skills are something which students are expected to pick up *en passant* while pursuing their course of study, or to already possess when they arrive at university, or some combination of the two, i.e., that they arrive sufficiently well prepared to be able to learn an unstated agenda of academic proficiencies together with a body of course content.

This may have been a sustainable strategy at some earlier time. When a much smaller proportion of the population went to university, and therefore university students represented the best prepared of their generation, and the societal resources which support higher education were not spread so thin, so that (for example) maintenance grants obviated the need for students to hold jobs, it may have been realistic to expect university students to learn a curriculum of academic discourse skills as a side dish to their studies.

Those circumstances no longer obtain, though, for the vast majority of teaching contexts. In western countries, a larger proportion of the population is attending university than ever before, not just the elite of each generation. A growing number of students are learning through the medium of a second or foreign language, adding an extra layer of difficulty to the academic writing task. In countries where the higher education sector has expanded, universities have a strong pressure to fill places, even if it means admitting students who have relatively poorer preconditions for success.

In this context, a model which expects students to develop skills in source use which they have not been explicitly taught in a systematic, thorough and adequately resourced way is a recipe for increasing the incidence of plagiarism. Holding them accountable for those skills, by detecting plagiarism and punishing offenders, is something like shooting the horses which fail to jump over the hurdle. It is a workable strategy if the only objective is to have a pool of horses which can make it over the hurdle and wastage is not an issue. However, that is not the mission of a higher education institution, nor a tenable position for one to be in.

Activity

Conducting an institutional audit. This chapter has identified areas in which university administration can act to prevent plagiarism. What is the situation at your university in each of these areas? What scope exists for improving them?

- Regulation and policy
- Information
- Detection
- Procedures
- Penalties

- Resourcing staff to teach source use
- Student resources to learn about writing and source use
- Coordination of instruction across subjects
- Staff support for plagiarism and source use
- Admissions criteria

Questions for discussion or reflection

1 This chapter suggested that policy at the university level is often concerned only with deceptive plagiarism and patchwriting and other non-deceptive source use issues are dealt with by the teacher. Does that match the reality at your institution? Is that an effective division of responsibility?

2 In a survey of Australian universities Sutherland-Smith found that it is regulated centrally and thus 'plagiarism is not something that is able to be defined or administered differently across the institution' (2010: 7). Is a central solution or a devolved one preferable?

3 Some institutions make the use of 'plagiarism-detection' software compulsory, in at least some circumstances. Is a decision of that nature one which should be made by university administration or teachers?

Part Three

Contextualising plagiarism

7

International students and second-language writers

Summary

It is frequently asserted that students whose first language is not English are more likely to plagiarise, or do so for reasons related to a different understanding of plagiarism prevalent in their home culture. This chapter presents and weighs up the evidence for and against such differences which has been presented in the research literature, and explores the aspects of the international student experience which have relevance for issues related to source use and plagiarism in academic writing. Other factors which are connected to plagiarism in the writing of international students include their language skills in conjunction with the heavy burden of writing academic texts in a second language, and the degree of experience with academic writing in any language with which they arrive at an English-medium university. The implications for teachers are discussed and the chapter concludes that while the knowledge and skills which international students need to avoid plagiarism and use sources effectively are not fundamentally different from those which any student needs, their starting points when arriving at university in the English-speaking world are more diverse, and support needs to be tailored accordingly.

When you have finished this chapter you will be better able to understand the needs and challenges of international students and be able to adjust your approach in the classroom to meeting them in ways which will be maximally effective in developing their knowledge and skills for good source use.

Many people believe that students who do not have English as a first language are especially likely to write in ways which are associated with plagiarism. Is that an idea you have heard, and if so, what explanations for it have been offered? The two quotations below present rather different perspectives on this question. Which matches your own experience most closely?

Korean students copy from various kinds of sources from books and magazines to Internet. . . . Western teachers get indignant over foreign students [*sic*] copying behavior . . . Asian students get then confused at these western teachers' emotionally charged reactions.

(Moon, 2002: 1351)

I know what plagiarism is. We have it in Korea too, and we take it seriously.

(Student quoted in Errey, 2002: 19)

An idea about plagiarism which is often heard, and which some appear to accept as a truism, is that students with English as a second or foreign language are more likely to plagiarise than others, but do so because of cultural differences which lead to them not perceiving plagiarism as wrong. Plagiarism is related on the one hand to values and on the other hand to language production; this is therefore an apparently plausible view. However, another well represented view challenges these proposed differences. After briefly outlining what is meant by second-language speakers and international students, this chapter will examine the arguments for and against differences in an understanding of plagiarism, or a proclivity to commit it, and then conclude with recommendations for good practice in handling plagiarism with this diverse group of writers.

International students and second-language writers: Who are they?

Much of the commentary and research which has addressed this question (and there is more of the former than the latter) has either conflated international students with second-language writers, or been based on groups of students who are both. They are, however, two distinct and only partly overlapping groups, each of which is quite heterogeneous.

The group of individuals studying through the medium of English[iv] as a foreign or second language is broad and diverse, and subsumes a number of distinctions related to language background and learning. The first of these is between English as a foreign language (EFL) and English as a second language (ESL), and the related distinction between language learning and language acquisition. When this distinction is observed (and it is not always), language learning refers to what happens with a foreign language in a classroom-based setting while acquisition is what happens in a more naturalistic setting, as for example the case of an immigrant who 'picks up' a language from exposure to it 'on the street'. While these categories are useful in that they indicate real differences in the mechanisms for and conditions around learning (or acquisition), they are not always distinct, as for example in the case of many international students, who have learned English as a classroom language in their home countries and then travel abroad to study entirely through the medium of English. These categories will therefore be conflated here, and the term 'second-language (L2) writer' will be used primarily because it is one most commonly used in the research literature on academic writing.

Another factor which distinguishes non-native speakers and can influence their experience of learning to produce academic texts in English is the context in which they have encountered the language. English has a global spread, but its status differs from country to country. A student from China may arrive at an English-speaking university having had years of classroom-based instruction in the language with an emphasis on grammar and vocabulary, but have limited experience using English for real communicative purposes. A student from India, on the other hand, may have had similar experiences, but alternatively may have been educated primarily or entirely in English, and possibly even had it as a home language. Students who immigrated to the English-speaking world during their primary or secondary education may have strong language skills by virtue of prolonged exposure to the language, but are likely not to be classified as international students if they completed secondary school in that country, with the result that the fact that they do not have native-like proficiency (if this is indeed the case) may not be visible in their enrolment records, etc.

As the last two examples indicate, there is not perfect overlap between international students and second-language speakers. Some international students may have grown up with the language, while some second-language speakers of English may, by virtue of permanent residence in a country, not be classed as international students. However, the overlap is substantial enough that for the purposes of this chapter the two terms will be used interchangeably.

The phenomenon of students from other countries and language backgrounds travelling to English-speaking countries such as the US, the UK and Australia is long-established. According to statistics from the Organisation for Economic Co-operation and Development, the number of non-citizen students in tertiary education in the UK rose from 209,550 in 1998 to 534,555 in 2010, and as early as 1991, commentators on the situation for international students in Australia noted that

> [ELL students] must be assessed by the same criteria as used for first language students, and yet the problems presented by their work are fundamentally different from those encountered in the work of native students
>
> (Ballard and Clanchy, 1991: 19)

The phenomenon of non-native speakers of English studying through the medium of English is, however, no longer confined to international students coming to countries like the US and the UK. Alternatives include distance courses and branch campuses of English-speaking universities in other countries. The British Council concluded in 2011, based on figures from the UK's Higher Education Statistics Agency, that the number of students studying in the UK had been outstripped by the number studying through UK institutions offshore.

Nor is the provision of English-medium courses the exclusive purview of the countries typically thought of as 'English-speaking'. In places such as the Netherlands and Scandinavia, English occupies a strong position generally, and is becoming the language of instruction on an increasing number of courses, making them attractive destinations for study. In 2008, according to OECD statistics, the five countries with the largest proportion of international students at their universities were, in descending order, Australia, Austria, the UK, Switzerland and New Zealand.

Outside of the traditional core of English-speaking countries, English is used at universities as part of what has been called a 'parallel-language environment', in which English is used in parallel with a local language. In one form, entire courses are taught in English; in other forms, English is a presence in some components of courses and assessment writing may be done in English. There are therefore many university students around the world who must learn to do academic writing – and therefore to use sources appropriately and effectively – in English. Given the widespread perception that L2 status contributes to textual plagiarism, it is important to understand the relationship between linguistic and cultural background on one hand, and plagiarism and source use on the other.

Plagiarism and L2 writers: What are the issues?

Two different aspects of the international student experience have been associated with an increased tendency to plagiarise. The first is cultural background in terms of the ideas, beliefs and values which vary across national boundaries. According to this explanation, the idea of plagiarism is understood differently in some cultures, or indeed is an alien concept altogether. Students who come from those countries therefore may not know what plagiarism is, or may not understand that it is considered a serious violation of academic ethics, or in some other way may not be able to understand the Anglo-Saxon perspective on plagiarism. A second explanation points to a specific feature of a culture, its educational system, and the fact that differences in educational practices can leave students unprepared for some of the tasks they will be required to take on at an English-medium university. The third explanation is that most international students have a first language which is not English, and therefore face challenges related to working through the medium of another language.

Cultural attitudes and perceptions of plagiarism

A frequently encountered idea is that international students simply are not equipped with an understanding of plagiarism, that 'in some cultural traditions plagiarism is not recognised as a sin: it is a normal academic practice to gather together what others have said into a sort of pastiche' (Cammish, 1997: 153). This explanation in its simplest form posits a simple lack of declarative knowledge. In a study of Hong Kong university students, only a small minority – four out of 170 – reported that the word 'plagiarism' had ever been explained to them (Deckert, 1993: 137). A knowledge gap like this is in principle something which could affect any student, regardless of cultural background, but a link is sometimes made with educational systems which, unlike those in the English-speaking world, do not perceive plagiarism as an issue worthy of classroom time:

> Korean students copy from various kinds of sources from books and magazines to Internet. And it has been allowed. More precisely, it has been ignored because plagiarism is not a concern of teachers in academic settings in Korea.
>
> (Moon, 2002: 1351)

A variation on this theme is that students may have heard a definition of plagiarism and know in theory that they are not supposed to do it, but lack a full awareness of the sorts of acts which must be avoided. This explanation, too, is one which could in principle apply to any student but the literature on plagiarism features many anecdotal accounts of international students in this position. Leki, for example, (1992) documented a case involving students who assumed that they could avoid plagiarism by memorising a text and reproducing it from memory, rather than directly from the printed page.

This possible difference is attributed to a variety of factors, one of which is a culturally specific orientation toward authority: that

> in a number of countries, particularly in Asia, there is considerable respect for the printed word and those in authority. Consequently, it is quite

normal for students to quote from authorities/books without feeling the need to acknowledge the source; nor is it necessarily expected.

(Jordan, 1997: 100)

This idea, that in some cultures 'humility is valued as a personal characteristic', is said to lead

many ESL composition students [to] hold fast to their image of themselves as students, tending to see themselves as apprentices and nonexperts, and not perceiving themselves as having any real authority, even over their own texts'

(Benson and Heidish, 1995: 322)

and has frequently been articulated as the source of the 'stereotype of the "plagiarizing overseas student"' (Ballard and Clanchy,1991: 3).

Another explanation is to do with cultural variation along a cline which has 'collective' orientations at one end and 'individual' at the other (e.g., Hofstede, 1984). In individualist cultures, it is said,

copying is an offence and dealt with as such. . . . To a student from a collectivist culture, however, there is nothing morally wrong with collusion. It does not contravene the moral code; indeed it may be construed as cooperation. In such a culture resources, including intellectual ones, are to be shared; opinions expressed are those of the group, not the individual.

(Barker, 1997: 115)

This idea was one issue covered in Deckert's (1993) investigation of Hong Kong students' knowledge about, and attitudes toward, plagiarism. While a similar study at a US university (Kroll, 1988) found that a quarter of students mentioned intellectual property rights as the most important reason for objecting to plagiarism, under 14% of Deckert's first-year university students gave a similar response, although the figure rose among third-year students.

Other cultural values or beliefs which have been suggested as an explanation include the idea that there is one, absolute truth, making citation unnecessary (since eternal truths are not the intellectual offspring of any particular person) and paraphrase dangerous (since, if the truth is absolute, altering the language in which it is expressed risks altering the facts). Deep respect for the teacher or other reader may dictate omitting references since the teacher, an expert in his or her field, will recognise the sources. Speaking of sources of plagiarism in Korean students' writing, Moon says that traditionally 'knowledge was confined to a small circle' which was

supposed to obtain knowledge from the approved authorities. It was shared knowledge. Therefore, even though there was no citation, a knowledgeable reader would figure out where the sources came from. And if a reader was not able to identify the source, it was his fault, which is the ignorance of his knowledge in the field.

(2002: 1353)

Although many of the culturally based explanations have contrasted Western and Eastern values, textual plagiarism by Italian students has been attributed to a cultural cause as well: specifically, the desire to produce a polished and smooth piece of writing has been connected with a general importance placed on making a good impression, a *bella figura* (Sherman, 1992).

There are, therefore, many voices arguing for the idea that cultural differences predispose L2 writers to write in a way which is likely to be called plagiarism. There is not universal agreement on this, however; in the second-language writing literature, assertions of cultural differences have been met by vocal disagreement, some of it from scholars embedded in the very cultures in which Western commentators have claimed these differences exist. According to a Vietnamese academic,

plagiarism is never allowed or made legitimate by Vietnamese culture or education. For example, even at primary school level, if a pupil copies another pupil's ideas to reproduce them in his/her very basic compositions (such as a description of one's favourite pet), his/her teachers and classmates will criticize and help that pupil realize that it is unacceptable to copy others' ideas for one's assessment purposes. Also, it is not unusual for school teachers to require students found plagiarizing to write down 100 times the same promise 'I will never steal others' ideas/writing again'. These practices show that plagiarism is viewed as unethical.

(Ha, 2006: 76)

A Chinese scholar takes essentially the same position:

Based on my educational experience as a native of China and the research I have conducted, I would like to argue that the claim that copying others' writing as one's own is allowed, taught and/or encouraged in China is not accurate.

(Liu, 2005: 235)

Students from the cultures concerned share this view, or appear to. In a study of Japanese university students, LoCastro and Masuko (2002: 22) found some students believed that cultural differences were real, saying for example that 'in Japan, people are not generally aware of plagiarism' but also found others who were upset when fellow students plagiarised, suggesting that they both were aware of plagiarism and held negative perceptions of it. Another study set in Japan (Wheeler, 2009) asked students to comment on a piece of writing which was clearly plagiarised, and they were highly critical of it. At a UK university, Errey (2002) found that staff offered culture as an explanation for plagiarism in their international students (as did staff in Australia in Bretag's 2004 study), but the students themselves distanced themselves from that explanation.

The difference between the views of staff and students may provide a partial understanding of why the idea of cultural causes for plagiarism is so persistent, despite reasons to be cautious about accepting them. Teachers who identify what looks like a form of cheating in the work of students they do not believe are cheaters search for a reason elsewhere, and culture is a convenient one. It is also a well intentioned one, and yet there is a need to be wary of it. Buranen notes that

> confident assertions like 'Asian students don't believe so and so' . . . are as inaccurate and misleading as any stereotype, and the effect is often condescending or patronizing, revealing an arrogance that says in essence, 'your culture is simple and transparent enough to be contained in a few pat phrases' . . .
>
> (Buranen, 1999: 73)

Bloch attributes a concurring view to Alton Becker: 'when you tell someone that they are different, they think you mean they are inferior' (2008: 220). A more practical danger in adopting the cultural-difference position is that the source of the problem is put down largely to knowledge: students from culture X do not know that plagiarism is wrong. A concomitant of that is that once they've been told 'don't plagiarise', staff members may see repeated problems with using sources as evidence of deceptive intent.

And yet for all the reasons not to rush headlong into adopting this explanation, a considerable body of literature persistently asserts that perceptions or experience of plagiarism vary across cultures (e.g., Hayes and Introna, 2005; Hirvela and Du, forthcoming; Rinnert and Kobayashi, 2005), making it difficult to discard the idea altogether. Is the cultural explanation right or wrong? The reality is very likely, as Bloch concludes, more complex than that:

> there is not today, nor ever has been, a single Chinese perspective on imitation, originality, and plagiarism, but . . . there is a different sense in how these concepts interact. Studying this relationship in a cross-cultural perspective reminds us of the danger of dichotomizing these concepts across cultures, so that only one culture is viewed as the 'other'.
>
> (2008: 228)

It may be then that the value of connecting plagiarism and culture is not that the latter can explain the former, but that the phenomenon of varied understandings of plagiarism, and approaches to using the words and ideas of others, can be a lens through which teachers can obtain a clearer view of the meaning of cultural differences and similarities in their relationship with their students.

Language and writing skills

An alternative connection between plagiarism and international students has considerably stronger support in the research literature: academic writing in a second language is a challenging task, and students who are not able to produce academic language which is as fluent as they would like it to be may rely on the language of their sources. Writing for assessment purposes is very common in the English-speaking world, but is not equally common everywhere (e.g., Bloch, 2001; Dryden, 1999; Hayes and Introna, 2005; Timm, 2007a; Timm, 2007b).

Nor is writing conceived of in similar terms around the world. It has been suggested that some educational systems encourage students to use memorisation or copying as a study practice (Matalene, 1985; Porte, 1995). An anecdotal account describes students from Malaysia being accused of plagiarism on an exam because they had memorised the textbook in preparation for the exam and were later able to produce extracts from it from memory (Leki, 1992). This story, offered as an illustration of different perspectives on plagiarism, demonstrates different abilities as well. It is difficult to imagine that many students from the US or the UK have such a facility for memorisation. If students are accustomed to such reproductive learning strategies, they may be likely to apply them to writing tasks.

In a detailed exposition of the instruction French students receive about writing and using sources, Donahue (2008) describes a system with an internal logic but one which emphasises different aspects of using sources than the Anglo-Saxon academic culture does. Students are taught to summarise, but their summaries can contain 'key phrases' (2008: 93) from the source without signalling them as quotation, and paraphrase is not only not the focus of instruction, it is actively discouraged with regard to literary texts. This serves as an example of the ways that international students' prior literacy practices can leave them ill-prepared for the sorts of academic writing they will do in the English-speaking world.

A range of factors in international students' academic backgrounds may therefore cause them to look favourably upon repeating the language of the source as a writing strategy, and by the same token they have an extra motivation for doing so. Most people, from undergraduates in their first term to senior and frequently published scholars, find academic writing challenging, because of the high degree of accuracy and precision of expression it requires. The ideas which academic texts express are often complex, and their language equally so. Producing academic writing in a second language only adds to the difficulty, and students frequently report that the desire to produce smooth texts and the perception, right or wrong, that they are unable to do so unaided, is a force leading them to use cut-and-paste strategies (e.g. Barks and Watts, 2001; Currie, 1998; Pecorari, 2008a).

One element in the problem is productive language abilities: having the skill to choose the words and structures which convey a message clearly, while avoiding errors in grammar or word choice. Receptive abilities also play a role, and in the case of source use, the ability to read in particular. Good reading skills are, naturally, necessary in order to be able to understand sources and texts (and understanding them is a precondition for being able to use them in effective ways, and to summarise and paraphrase appropriately and without distorting the meaning). Reading in a second language also takes more time (e.g., Shaw and McMillion, 2008), with the inevitable result that less time is available for writing.

It is worth stressing that the pressures of working in a second language are not felt only by those who are inadequately prepared for it. The language proficiency of prospective international students coming to an English-medium university is most frequently benchmarked against one of two instruments, the Test of English as a Foreign Language (TOEFL) or the International English Language Testing System (IELTS). A common minimum score for university admissions is 6.0 on the IELTS (corresponding approximately to 550 on the paper-based TOEFL or 80 on the Internet-based test). Some universities and programmes accept lower scores still. The band descriptors for the IELTS say that a score of 6.0 indicates a 'competent user' who

> has generally effective command of the language despite some inaccuracies, inappropriacies and misunderstandings. Can use and understand fairly complex language, particularly in familiar situations.

However, few students wish to hand in an essay – much less a dissertation or thesis – with 'some inaccuracies, inappropriacies and misunderstandings'. Most students aspire higher than that. They want their written work not only to avoid grammatical errors, but to sound like a scholarly work; they want to make use of the stock of phrases and expressions which characterise the academic texts which they are reading. In this respect they are no different from writers with English as a first language, but they have further to go to close the gap between their current skills and those they need to develop. Seen from this perspective, patchwriting can be seen to serve an important function for the L2 writer.

This view was widespread among the Hong Kong science students interviewed by Flowerdew and Li. They actively searched for models of 'repeatable' language, because the obstacles to composing a piece of research writing in English from scratch were insuperable:

> The first draft – we have to build up a framework – make it look like a paper; if you write it all by yourself, you definitely cannot produce a paper if you all do it by yourself . . . we may take from different sources, synthesize them, and express our own meaning. If we see a particularly good expression, we'll definitely use it.
>
> (2007: 450)

Disregarding for a moment concerns about plagiarism, this is likely to be an effective strategy for producing good writing, at the level of language. It is also likely to be an effective strategy for their future learning; the efficacy of repetition in language learning is well established. However, English L2 researchers caught in public plagiarism scandals (e.g., Li and Xiong, 1996) would probably advise these students not to disregard concerns about plagiarism; accusations can be fatally damaging to a scholarly career. Yet many L2 writers distinguish between copying 'good expressions' and appropriating results, and feel licensed to do the former provided they avoid the latter. Two Chinese researchers who were accused of plagiarism in a case reported in *Nature* offered this explanation: '"There is a significant degree of identity in the wording", they admitted, but the charge of plagiarism is not valid "because we have all the original data"' (Li and Xiong, 1996: 337). For writers in their position, a prohibition against patchwriting is perceived as a tax on being a second-language writer.

Implications for teachers

This chapter has highlighted some of the aspects of plagiarism which have particular resonance for international students. The role of cultural differences is contested, but the possibility that they contribute to an understanding of plagiarism cannot be discounted. On the other hand, skills in using sources as part of academic writing, and language skills more generally are undoubtedly an important issue. They exert opposing pressures to shape a difficult situation for the second-language writer. On the one hand, study through the medium of a second language adds to the already considerable demands of learning to write academic texts. On the other hand, their previous educational background may have put them further away from the finish line from the outset.

What does this mean for teachers who have international students and diagnose, or want to prevent, textual plagiarism in their work? International students need clear explanations of, and illustrations of plagiarism

- to know how textual plagiarism is handled at their university;
- to know what expectations teachers have of their source use, including the writer's responsibility to use sources transparently;
- to have support in learning the skills which are necessary to source use, but which are made more difficult by the fact of working through a second language, including (but not limited to) reading academic texts; reformulating ideas from them; using reporting verbs; etc.
- to have opportunities for practice, feedback and revision;
- to be met by teachers who understand that textual plagiarism can have non-deceptive causes, and are thus willing to extend the presumption of innocence to them.

In short, international students need nothing which home students do not; they simply need more of it, and tailored to their ability level, which may not be that of first-language speakers.

However, despite the fact that there are clear and undoubted costs working through the medium of a second language, particularly when carrying out the rhetorically complex tasks of which assessment writing consists, it does not always follow from that that second-language writers are necessarily in a deficit position with respect to their first-language peers. International students are a diverse group, and their diverse backgrounds may have equipped them with beneficial knowledge, skills and perspectives which their home-country counterparts lack. Further, the clearest sources of problems for international students are those linked to the difficulties of producing academic discourse. However, this is not an issue unique to them. Producing academic writing is part of entering academic culture, and plagiarism can be one of the consequences of this 'culture clash' for any novice academic writer. This is a theme that will be returned to in Chapter 9.

Activity

Documenting the situation for international students. This investigation consists of two parts: documenting rules and procedures, and interviewing an international student about perceptions and experiences. First, use your university's website, or contact the admissions office, to find out:

- What admissions criteria apply to students who have a first language other than English (or than the language of instruction at your institution)? Which test(s) are accepted as a measure of English proficiency and what score do students need to achieve on it?
- Are there any groups of international students or second-language users who are not required to provide a test score?

Next, interview a student with English (or your institution's teaching language) as a foreign language.

- Why was he or she motivated to study at your institution?
- Before beginning this course, how much experience had he or she had of using English in daily life? And in academic settings?
- Before starting this course, how much experience had he or she had of assessment writing? In which language(s) was it done?
- How difficult or easy is it to study through the medium of another language? What about listening to and understanding lectures? Doing assigned reading? Doing coursework?

- What score did that student get on the English proficiency test used for admissions?

Questions for discussion or reflection

1 What are the language backgrounds of your students? Is it possible to group them into the categories international student/home student or first-language/second-language user, or do the categories blur?
2 Do the reading section from a sample IELTS test (http://www.ielts.org/ test_takers_information/test_sample/academic_reading_sample.aspx)   in the time specified in the instructions. How does the difficulty of the task compare to the reading you assign or recommend to your students? If English is your first language, imagine taking a test like this in the foreign language which you know best. Would your skills be sufficient?
3 As discussed in this chapter, there is a widespread belief that cultural differences may make it more likely that international students plagiarise. If this is the case, to what extent might it be appropriate to respond differently to plagiarism by international and home students?

8

Differences across academic subjects

Summary • Writing in the disciplines • How are sources cited? • Signalled and unsignalled quotation • Learning to meet disciplinary conventions • Disciplinary variation in a broader perspective • Activity • Questions for discussion or reflection

Summary

Academic integrity policies tend to disregard the differences between the academic disciplines (especially with regard to plagiarism) and the features of academic texts that are valued and conventional. As a result, institutions routinely have a single set of university-wide plagiarism policies. Examples of the differences in source use and what constitutes good academic writing practice across the academic disciplines are used in this chapter to illustrate the nature and scale of the variations. Examples that reveal different points of view between members of the same disciplines and different disciplines on the significance of copied text, given where it is within the submission, and the extent to which the copied text diminishes the original work are provided.

This examination indicates a gap between one-size-fits all policies and great variation across subject areas, and a conclusion reached in this chapter is that staff and students both would be better served either by a greater consistency over subject borders, or by policies which are sensitive to the differences which exist. Either is likely to be an improvement over the existing situation.

When you have finished this chapter you will have a sense of the ways in which the source-use practices of your subject area differ from those in other parts of the university community. You will be able to form a view as to whether your institution and subject area are better served by university-wide plagiarism policies, and be able to contribute effectively to this debate at your institution.

Because university-wide plagiarism policies tend to be couched in general terms, it is easy to miss specific differences in practices across subject areas. Consider how well the two quotations below reflect your experiences.

I first heard it when we revised our academic integrity policy a few years after I started teaching at my small liberal arts college, but I didn't comprehend the significance. I heard it again later in response to various cases brought to the Academic Integrity Committee by colleagues across the disciplines. What is interesting to me is that none of my colleagues said it directly until I sat down to talk one-on-one with them. When I did that, this is what they said: *Most of these rules about how to use and cite sources don't actually apply in my discipline.*

(Jamieson, 2008: 77)

All 18 universities in the study have consistently located plagiarism in disciplinary or academic misconduct regulations of university policy provisions. Plagiarism management processes are generally passed by the Academic Board or Academic Council of each university and therefore have university-wide standing and apply to all staff and students across the particular institution. Hence, plagiarism is not something that is able to be defined or administered differently across the institution, and there is an expectation in the discourse of the regulations that there is consistency in managing plagiarism across faculties, schools and departments.

(Sutherland-Smith, 2010: 7)

The two quotations above indicate an existing gap between the fact that academic integrity policies tend to be colour-blind to academic discipline (especially with respect to plagiarism) and the very real differences across disciplines in the ways that sources are used. This gap is important to understand for several reasons. An awareness of practices within the subject area is necessary in order to be able to help students learn what they may and may not do with sources. This is especially important for individuals who come from another subject area, and in educational contexts in which students take courses across the curriculum. To the extent that some regulation and handling of source use and plagiarism (e.g., the shaping of policy) happens at a university-wide level, an awareness of cross-subject differences is essential to shaping good policy and regulatory practices. The implications of differences across subject areas, for teachers and policy makers, are discussed at the end of the chapter.

A handful of studies have investigated the question of whether there are differences in the proclivity of students to plagiarise, and appear to give reason to believe that this might be an issue of especial importance for students in the STEM disciplines (Science, Technology, Engineering and Math). Selwyn (2008) surveyed university students in the UK about the frequency with which they had engaged in acts representing various sorts of plagiarism, ranging from copying small chunks of text to purchasing an assignment. He found significant differences in the frequency of these acts across subject areas, with a general trend for students from the arts and humanities to report less plagiarism with those in the STEM areas reporting more. Julliard's (1994) study was primarily interested in the area of medicine, but some respondents from the English subject were surveyed, and reported that they were less likely to use sources in ways that could be considered plagiarism.

McCullough and Holmberg (2005) searched phrases from master's dissertations on Google to test the usefulness of the search engine as a tool for finding plagiarism and discovered the greatest frequency of copied language in the STEM fields, and lowest in the arts and humanities. In a corpus investigation which compared master's dissertations and PhD theses with the sources they used, the STEM texts (and those from the natural sciences in particular) contained more textual plagiarism (Pecorari, 2006).

More tentatively, there are suggestions that plagiarism may occur especially frequently in the work of business students. McCullough and Holmberg's (2005) study found that business students, whom they grouped together with the social scientists, fell between STEM subjects and the arts in the frequency with which they copied language from their sources. Selwyn (2008) reported differences among groups in the types of behaviour they reported engaging in, and found that business students were most likely to purchase or copy an entire assignment, but less likely than students in some other fields to engage in smaller-scale copying (a difference which may come about in part because copying entire texts removes the occasion for copying smaller parts of it). However, an investigation of cheating behaviour generally, including some types of plagiarism, found business students reported engaging in those behaviours less often (Iyer and Eastman, 2006). Another study which compared students in psychology and business did not directly address cheating or plagiarism but did ask about behaviour such as sharing assignments with friends, which could easily lead to it (Sutton and Taylor, 2011). There was an overall *in*frequent reporting of problematic behaviours, but it was lower among business students than the psychology students.

There is, therefore, reason to believe that subject area is an important element in understanding plagiarism, but what, precisely, is its role? Is the conclusion to be drawn that STEM students are more likely to cheat, or more likely to be patchwriters? While there is evidence for differences in the ways writers use sources across subject areas, there is much less support for any conclusions about the causes of these differences (and specifically for the idea that the frequency of *prototypical* plagiarism varies across subjects). This chapter explores some of the differences across academic cultures which can shed light on these patterns, and then concludes by outlining the implications for teachers and administrators.

Writing in the disciplines

In his classic work *Academic tribes and territories,* Tony Becher gives an anthropological treatment to the study of academic disciplines, showing how differences in approaches across the academy relate to differences in the way knowledge is produced and the approaches to understanding which are valued. He draws on a population-density metaphor to describe one of the key disciplinary differences, describing 'urban' and 'rural' research areas. Urban areas are densely populated; there are relatively many researchers in these areas in relation to the topics available. This population density creates a pressure to produce findings quickly (before someone else does), thus creating a need for channels of publication which disseminate findings rapidly. In rural fields the competition for research topics is not as great, and thus the pace of publication is not as frantic. There is a rough if imperfect correspondence between urban areas and the STEM subjects, and rural areas and the arts and humanities. Not surprisingly, these differences are seen in the forms of publication which are held to be most conventional or prestigious. For example, in the natural sciences, research articles – which offer the fastest route for disseminating research findings – are a dominant form of publication and monographs less so, at least in research writing, while in the humanities the proportions are more balanced, or even – in some subjects – reversed.

The disciplinary preference for certain forms of publication is reflected, logically enough, in the types of sources cited. A study of disciplinary variation in citation in dissertations and theses (Pecorari, 2006) found that in biology (an urban area), over 80% of the publications cited were research articles, while that figure was approximately 20% in engineering, the humanities and social sciences. In the other fields, monographs and anthologies were more frequently cited (and in engineering, reports and standards). These differences in student writing approximate the trends in published writing. An informal examination of five articles from recent issues of a journal in biology and five from a journal in literary history for the purposes of this chapter showed that 95% of the sources cited in biology were research articles, as opposed to only 17% in literary history. Forty per cent of sources in the latter field were monographs, and approximately a quarter were the primary sources which were the object of inquiry in the article, the raw data on which the research it reported was based.

The specific contours of various publication forms differ as well, with journal articles being shorter in the STEM disciplines and longer in the 'soft' fields. An examination of recent articles in a journal in biology (*Mycopathologia*) and one in linguistics (*Applied Linguistics*) showed that the average length of articles was 2,692 words and 7,569 words, respectively. The explanation usually given for this difference is the relative need for discussion. At the risk of generalising, the STEM fields deal in objective fact, and it is the facts themselves which matter; the form in which they are expressed is much less important. Consider the following examples from research articles in biology and linguistics, respectively:

Example 8.1

It was further shown that resistant transformants could be generated by integration of a single copy of a CalMH3 gene, derived from a MPA-resistant strain (Beckerman *et al.* 2001). CalMH3R has been used as a marker gene for integrative transformation in C. albicans (Staib *et al.* 1999; Wirsching *et al.* 2000; Beckerman *et al.* 2001), C. tropicalis (Beckerman *et al.* 2001) and C. dubliniensis (Staib *et al.* 2000).

Example 8.2

In a provocative paper, which served to open up the field of gender and humor from a sociolinguistic point of view, Jenkins (1985) claims that women's humor is cooperative, inclusive, supportive, integrated, spontaneous, and self-healing, while men's humor is exclusive, challenging, segmented, pre-formulated, and self-aggrandizing – claims which Crawford (1989:161) notes are "strikingly congruent" with her respondents' self reports.

Although the two are approximately equal in length, Example 8.1 reports content from more sources but says less about each, while Example 8.2 does the opposite. The first fits in references to six earlier works. The information reported from them is, in the case of the first source, an unqualified assertion about one of its findings, and in the case of the others, the approach they took. On the other hand, 8.2 refers to just two sources, but provides more interpretation about each. The first, for example, is categorised as 'provocative' and its place is the field of research is related, as well as one of its central claims, while the second source is related to the first. The need to provide commentary at this level is one of the factors which makes the appearance of sources – in this case, the relative lengths of examples of the same genre, the research article – different across fields.

An implication of these differences in the types of sources used and their superficial contours is that the information-searching and reading processes of students differ across disciplines, or at least should do if they are to produce writing which is consistent with the conventions of their fields of study. Students in the humanities may begin the search for sources of information on a topic in the library catalogue in the reasonable expectation that they will find books on the topic, but students in the sciences will need to consult databases which index or contain articles from academic journals, while engineers may need to find professional standards or technical reports from different databases still. The differences in the length of sources, and the varying degrees of discursivity which explain some of it, also have implications for the reading process both in terms of the time students may have to spend on it, and the degree of attention they need to bring to understanding finer nuances.

How are sources cited?

Significant differences exist across academic disciplines in how sources are used, how that use is signalled, and even how conventions are codified. Writers in the humanities and social sciences are often asked to prepare texts in accordance with the instructions in one of a number of detailed style manuals, such as the *APA Publication Manual, the MLA Handbook for Writers of Research Papers* or the *Chicago Manual of Style*. These give comprehensive explanations of style conventions, including instructions for formatting in-text references and reference-list entries. By contrast, writers in STEM subjects are often referred to the style of an influential organisation (e.g., IEEE) or publication (e.g., *Nature*), and these are typically much less detailed; for example, the section of the *Nature* 'manuscript formatting guide' devoted to the format of references is less than 400 words long. This difference in level of detail reflects the fact that references occur in more varied forms in the humanities and social sciences.

Citations can appear in a text in more or less prominent positions. In Example 8.1 above, all of the references are relegated to parentheses, and while they serve an important function in alerting the reader to the source of the information, the text would be equally readable without the references, as 8.3 illustrates. References of this sort are what are called non-integral citations, and can be contrasted with integral citations (Swales, 1990) in which the source is named in a way that makes it an inherent part of the citing sentence, as in 8.2, where Jenkins claims something, and Crawford notes something.

Example 8.3

It was further shown that resistant transformants could be generated by integration of a single copy of a CaIMH3 gene, derived from a MPA-resistant strain. CaIMH3R has been used as a marker gene for integrative transformation in C. albicans, C. tropicalis and C. dubliniensis.

Example 8.4

The insect immune system demonstrates a number of structural and functional similarities to the innate immune system of mammals [1] and, as a consequence, insects can be utilised as models for assessing the virulence of a variety of microbial pathogens [2, 3].

Example 8.5

Plasmids were introduced into *S. cerevisiae* as described [22]. *C. albicans* genomic DNA was prepared according to [10].

In Example 8.4, which uses a system of numbered references common in the STEM fields, the sources are still less prominent, by virtue of their names being absent. Although it is not impossible to combine a numbering system with integral references (as Example 8.5 shows), it is less common. Integral citations on the other hand require the writer to make a set of subsidiary choices about which reporting verb, or other reporting language, to use (see Chapter 4). Saying that Jenkins 'claims' something about differences in women's and men's use of humour acknowledges that the idea, while founded on data, requires interpretation, and therefore different interpretations may exist. It also leaves the option open to the writer at a later point to challenge the claim, while an alternative, such as 'as Jenkins notes', would imply that the writer agrees with Jenkins, and make it impossible to challenge the idea without appearing self-contradictory.

It is therefore not surprising that disciplinary differences in the use of these forms of citation exist. In one study, 90% of citations in biology were non-integral, compared to 65% in sociology and 35% in philosophy (Hyland, 2004). The subjective humanities subjects take advantage of the opportunities which integral citations offer to evaluate the strength of a proposition from a source, hedge the writer's commitment to it, etc., while the fact-oriented STEM subjects can content themselves with attributing a proposition to its source. A reference like the one in Example 8.6 would not be improved by recasting it as has been done in 8.6a and 8.6b to introduce evaluative reporting verbs.

Example 8.6

The measurement of contact angles, formed by sessile drops of three different liquids (two polar and one apolar), enables the calculation of the surface free energy and the degree of hydrophobicity (van Oss 1997).

Example 8.6a

Van Oss (1997) argues that the measurement of contact angles formed by sessile drops of three different liquids (two polar and one apolar), enables the calculation of the surface free energy and the degree of hydrophobicity.

Example 8.6b

Van Oss (1997) subscribes to the view that the measurement of contact angles formed by sessile drops of three different liquids (two polar and one apolar), enables the calculation of the surface free energy and the degree of hydrophobicity.

This difference in the degree of subjectivity in a research area, and the concomitant need (or lack of a need) to hedge, qualify and attenuate claims, is also responsible for what is perhaps the most striking difference in citation across disciplines, the use of quotation. In the STEM disciplines quotation – the signalled repetition of a wording from the source – is used so rarely as to be virtually non-existent. In the social sciences it is an unsurprising feature but often – depending on the research topic – less frequently used than paraphrase or summary. In some publications in the humanities, by contrast, quotation is the most common form of reference to a source.

These observable differences in the ways that writers incorporate references to their sources across disciplines have significant implications for students learning to write academic texts in their area of study. Students in the humanities and social sciences have a broader menu of conventional options open to them. They can quote or paraphrase or summarise, use integral or non-integral citations, and make use of a wide range of reporting verbs. This gives them considerable latitude to make choices which will be effective in helping them accomplish their textual purposes, but each of these choices implies the need to learn to use a linguistic tool, so the rhetorical demands on writers in the soft fields are higher.

Writers in STEM subjects have a diametrically opposed set of constraints and aids. They do not need to develop the ability to distinguish between nuanced degrees of commitment to choose appropriately among 'Jenkins suggests', 'Jenkins posits' and 'Jenkins supports the idea that'. Neither do they need to debate with themselves whether a paraphrase is appropriate, or whether the proposition to be reported from a source is so sensitive that the words of the author need to be quoted to avoid the possibility of distortion. Direct quotation is rarely likely to be needed. By the same token, writers in these areas do not have the option of falling back on openly signalled quotation when they feel the challenges of finding their own wordings are too great.

Signalled and unsignalled quotation

The brief review of research into disciplinary variation in textual plagiarism with which this chapter began showed that there is reason to think that writers in STEM subjects may be more likely to plagiarise. Not only do they report engaging in specific acts identified as plagiarism, text-based studies have identified more unattributed copying from sources in their work. Do those findings reflect a greater proclivity in some disciplines to cheat, or a different understanding across disciplines about what constitutes plagiarism? It was seen in earlier chapters that great individual diversity exists in terms of which source-dependent writing strategies are considered legitimate and which are considered plagiarism. Do cross-disciplinary patterns exist in this respect?

Although too little is known about this, the available evidence would indicate that the answer may be 'yes'. If so, it is likely that a source of these differences lies in understandings of what is an original creation and therefore the intellectual property of its creator, and what is so widely known or available that if it were to be attributed to any given individual, deciding which individual to attribute it to would be both difficult and unrewarding.

This can be illustrated by thinking about the introductions to research articles, which is where a great many (though by no means all) references to sources appear. In the examples seen earlier the choices to be made about how to refer to sources in Example 8.2 had a potentially greater impact on the conclusions the reader would draw about those sources than Example 8.1. This points to one sort of originality in the review of earlier research: the writer makes a series of active decisions about how to portray propositions from the source. In some areas, particularly those which are inherently multi-disciplinary, there are decisions with real significance to be made as well about which existing literature should be reported. Framing an article on the use of humour primarily in the literature of pragmatics would put the emphasis on the effects of the language in use. Introducing the literature from sociolinguistics which deals with differences in how men and women communicate more generally gives the work a gendered perspective with an entirely different set of implications. All of these aspects require the writer to make choices which influence the shape the rest of the article will take, and therefore the impact the findings will have on the literature, and any two writers approaching the same task would be likely to produce rather different introductions. In that sense, the introduction to an article can be seen as a creative work, worthy of attribution.

This is not a view which is universally shared, though, and there is reason to think that some of the differences are related to disciplinary perspective. When a group of Turkish scientists were accused of plagiarism on a large scale, their response was that the textual plagiarism in their articles, which they did not deny, was insignificant because it came from the introductions of other works:

> Borrowing sentences in the part of a paper that simply helps to better introduce the problem should not be seen as plagiarism. Even if our introductions are not entirely original, our results are – and these are the most important part of any scientific paper.
>
> (Yilmaz, 2007: 658)

A similar view was echoed by a student in biology who used a patchwriting strategy extensively in a literature review. She explained that she had been careful to attribute ideas to the relevant source whenever they were the author's own research findings, but felt that the content of introductions were 'kind of like common knowledge that most people know' and that it was therefore appropriate to copy it without attribution (Pecorari, 2008a: 116). Contrasting this, another biology student explained a reference to an article which he had not read, but felt obliged to cite. The article described (he said) the composition of a medium which the student had used for cultures in his experiments. He believed that his practice in citing the article but not reading it was common, and had a logical explanation: the medium itself was commercially available, and the laboratory he worked in purchased it ready-made. There was, therefore, no real reason to read the article that described the making of it. However, the researchers who had developed it had done something creative and original and should be credited with it.

These researchers are articulating a distinction between ideas and knowledge which is not always found in the social sciences and especially the humanities; indeed, it does not reflect a distinction which is always meaningful in those subjects. In some research paradigms the act of expressing an analysis (the research method) of a text (the research material) are themselves the research findings: separating them is impossible. An implication for source use and textual plagiarism is that if language and content are inextricably intertwined, then all textual plagiarism represents a transgression of an author's proprietorial rights. If they can be separated, however, then language which is used to express 'unoriginal' content may be free for the taking.

This was very much the view taken by a senior scientist who was interviewed about plagiarism and source use as part of a study of staff attitudes. He expressed a desire that, in the interests of learning to produce good writing, he wished his students and post-doctoral researchers would attempt fewer original words and do more copying of certain types of language:

> they've read quite a lot but that's reflected surprisingly little in their own [texts] – they come up with their own strange formulations when they've read descriptions of this a hundred times for sure, why do they write such funny stuff themselves? So I'm surprised that people don't . . . make use of functional text, so to speak.
>
> (Pecorari and Shaw, 2012: 154)

This scientist was talking about the sort of formulaic language which was discussed in Chapter 1:

From this it can be concluded that . . .
Little research to date has explored . . .
The strains used are shown in Table 1.
Results were considered statistically significant at the .05 level.

It would be hard to argue that any of these are the original creation of any single writer who should be credited for them. The four phrases above return many, many hits on Google (the first is found nearly 1,300,000 times, for example!). Nor would paraphrasing be an advantage; neither of the following would be an improvement, although they would be decidedly original:

When we saw that there were results at the .05 level, we considered them statistically significant.
It was necessary to establish a threshold of statistical significance, and .05 was it.

While formulaic language is found in all discourse, there is reason to think that it may be a particularly common phenomenon in the STEM subjects. The frequency of such language, in combination with the fact that quotation is not used in these fields, presents a number of problems for students in those subjects. They have more incentive to copy without attribution than their peers in other subjects, because copying with attribution – quoting – is not an option to them. However, while some academic gatekeepers, such as the scientist quoted above, would endorse this approach, others would categorise it as plagiarism.

Another problem is how they are expected to learn what can and cannot be done with sources. That, and how teachers can help, are the topics of the next section.

Learning to meet disciplinary conventions

Earlier in this chapter, variation in disciplinary conventions for source use were described and connected to the values and orientations toward research and knowledge which distinguish academic disciplines. These observations make explicit something which, for most academic writers at all levels, is implicit and rarely consciously observed. Experienced scientists do not mull over the choice to quote or not and reject it as running counter to the conventions in their fields; they have internalised those conventions. For experienced academic writers, making the choices which lead to texts which conform to disciplinary conventions is instinctive at least as much as it is the result of conscious decisions.

Inexperienced academic writers learn what is conventional in part by producing texts and receiving feedback on them, and in large part by reading the works of published scholars in their field, and observing, both consciously and unconsciously how those texts are written. However, some aspects of source use are more observable than others. One area of difference noted above was a tendency to cite books in the humanities and avoid them in the sciences. This is a tendency which novice academic writers can easily observe from the reference lists of the works they read. The same is not equally true, however, for features such as language repeated from a source, for the reason which was pointed out in an earlier chapter: some aspects of source use can only be observed if the source and the new text which cites it are seen side-by-side.

The fact that many authors include signalled quotation can alert a writer in sociology to the fact that quotation is a commonly used tool in that field. The fact that quotation marks are conspicuous by their absence in biology will probably alert students in biology to the fact that signalled quotation is not used. However, if an author has carefully paraphrased and avoided repeating language from a source, there are no overt signals of that fact. Inexperienced academic writers are forced to draw their own conclusions about appropriate intertextual relationships, and the evidence is that they often draw the wrong conclusions. The absence of quotation marks may indicate that language has *not* been repeated from a source, but it may be interpreted by inexperienced writers as indicating that quotations do not need to be signalled.

The same problem affects teachers working with student writing. If a student refers exclusively to very old sources, a teacher who knows there are more recent works on the topic will be likely to spot the problem and direct the student to newer literature. If a student uses signalled quotation in a way which is unconventional, again, that can be observed, and can be the subject of feedback. But patchwriting often goes undiagnosed, and the result is that the student interprets the absence of feedback as confirmation that that is an appropriate strategy.

There are several things teachers can do to help students learn about the ways that sources are and are not conventionally used in their disciplines. One is to make those conventions explicit, and describe the things that students can, should, and should not do when writing from sources. This can be done effectively not only by telling, but by letting them discover. Giving students a reading list and a set of questions ('How does the writer signal that content comes from a source?' 'What sort of sources has the writer used?') will make the process of learning by observation more conscious, and therefore more effective.

Although some aspects of source-use conventions are arbitrary (there is no particularly important principle behind the choice to use 'p.' to indicate a page number or to omit it), many have reasons behind them. In respect of those aspects of source use which vary across disciplines, some of those reasons have been discussed in this chapter. Explaining the function of highly evaluative reporting verbs or quotation, and the reasons they are or are not important rhetorical tools in your field will help underscore an important message about references to sources: they are not primarily empty formalities, they exist to help the text in which they appear achieve its purpose.

Because any individual teacher's view of an appropriate way to use sources may not match that of the teacher in the next room, giving good advice to students involves speaking to your colleagues and ensuring to the greatest extent possible that any instructions or advice given to students will serve them across their educations, and not just in the framework of a specific assignment or class. Where that is not possible, the fact that instructions have limited applicability, and the rules of the game may be changed in another class, or term, or type of assignment, should be acknowledged, and the reasons for it given.

Disciplinary variation in a broader perspective

This chapter has devoted considerable space to describing differences in source use across subject areas. In addition to helping show how teachers can help their students learn about the conventions of their subject area, there are several other important implications of the differences. One is that teachers need to be aware of the assumptions that students may bring to the classroom if they have previously studied in other fields. In other words, not only do teachers need to help students discover the standards and conventions for source use which apply in the subject, they need to be aware that students may have another, contradictory set of beliefs about good practice which they learned somewhere else.

In addition, source use and plagiarism often arise as issues at a university-wide level. A teacher who sits on a disciplinary panel, or who brings a case of plagiarism to a disciplinary panel, or who is appointed to a committee to review the university's policy on plagiarism, needs to be aware that what his or her colleagues will see as good practice, or as transgressive, will depend in part upon the academic area from which they come.

The diversity of practices described in this chapter raises the question of whether university-wide policies and procedures are in fact appropriate. Jamieson, quoted at the beginning of this chapter, relates how after having heard of cross-subject variation from many of her colleagues, she suggested shaping policy tailored to specific subject areas. She got a vocal negative response: her colleagues felt that even though the university-wide policy was a poor fit for their subjects, it was better than no central regulation at all.

In addition, while subject area explains some of the differences in understandings about plagiarism and source use, part of it arises from different understandings on the part of individuals within those disciplines. It would therefore be premature to call for subject-specific policies. It is not, however, premature to suggest that the idea be discussed within our universities and departments; that indeed, is greatly overdue. At present different standards and expectations are in place across the university, with the result that teachers respond to student work, and assess it, and even label it as plagiarism, inconsistently.

A discussion which acknowledges and exposes our differences on the subject of what constitutes plagiarism and good source use could conclude that greater harmonisation is needed, or it could end up with a resolve that the academic subject areas should each go their own ways. Without advocating either solution, it seems that both would be an improvement on the current situation of largely unacknowledged differences and the inconsistencies they permit.

Activity

Disciplinary conventions for source use. Draw on your understanding of practices in your field and say whether the following are acceptable and conventional features of academic writing. Are these things that a) occur often? b) occur sometimes? c) occur rarely? d) are questionable or not acceptable, but are not plagiarism? e) are plagiarism?

- using an author-date referencing system
- using a referencing system of numbered end notes
- referring to sources more than ten years old
- referring to sources more than fifty years old
- citing newspaper articles
- citing web pages
- quoting from a source by repeating language verbatim and putting it in quotation marks
- repeating language from the introduction of an article but not using quotation marks

Now look at a research article in your field which you consider to be well written. Imagine a student reading that article and deducing rules about source use from it. Which of the conventions you identified above could be deduced from the article? Which could not?

Questions for discussion or reflection

1 How did you learn the things you know about how to write academic texts in your discipline? Which things were you told, and by whom? Which things did you observe from other people's writing, and to what extent were those observations conscious or unconscious?

2 Identify half a dozen conventions for academic writing in your field, and imagine how you would explain them to a student. Which ones, if any, are arbitrary, and which have significance.

3 Have you ever encountered a student who experienced difficulty due to encountering different source use practices in different subjects or departments? How was the difficulty exposed? How did you explain the practices in your subject to the student?

9

Diversity and change

Summary

The student population is becoming increasingly heterogeneous and learning in different ways. Non-traditional students lack exposure to academic literacy before they arrive at university, and the new demands of both reading the subject and developing good academic writing skills can present serious challenges for them. The millennial generation who have been brought up with constant access to the Internet, mobile communications and social media applications, and who routinely cut and paste and forward text in their normal day-to-day communications, can find the formal citation conventions a serious and unfamiliar imposition. The increasing cost of tertiary education is one factor which has made distance learning a more attractive option, and for some, the only practical way to obtain a university education. The opportunities for teachers to impart the understanding and skills of good source use as part of distance learning can be more limited still than in traditional classroom-based instruction. There is the potential for a 'perfect storm' with an increasing number of non-traditional students from the millennial generation electing to study on a distance basis. This underscores the necessity of being proactive in introducing opportunities to teach effective source use and build opportunities for practice into all courses, regardless of the mode of instruction.

When you have finished this chapter you will understand the aspects of writing academic texts and using sources in conventional and effective ways which are particularly impacted by the heterogeneity which increasingly characterises higher education in many contexts worldwide.

Student background has often been offered as an explanatory factory for plagiarism. The quotation below takes up one aspect of background which may be implicated in this issue. What others are relevant in your experience?

It is clear that the students whom I interviewed had very little previous experience in writing from multiple sources. Their dominant experience was in descriptive or narrative composition . . . Only those who achieved high marks in their essays . . . reported any experience of writing from multiple sources, with the exception of Mangalisu. I think it follows logically from these prior educational experiences in writing, that students will encounter enormous difficulty in the genres of the academic essay, where they are expected to integrate multiple sources, and, underlying that, to have some understanding of knowledge as constructed, with multiple viewpoints and perspectives being possible.

(Angélil-Carter, 2000: 102)

Today's university students are a diverse group in terms of their backgrounds, their motivations, their experiences and their preparation, and are learning in diverse ways at university. This chapter looks at three aspects of that diversity which present fundamental challenges to how we teach about plagiarism and source use.

Generalisations are always dangerous, and this chapter engages in more than a few. This is not to trivialise the students it attempts to describe, or suggest that all students fit in neat boxes labelled with their key characteristics and group memberships, and it certainly is not to suggest that teachers should meet their students as representatives of a group, rather than as individuals. The purpose of this chapter is to paint a portrait of the characteristics which many university students share, so that it can inform our understanding of the individuals we meet in the (real or virtual) classroom. What are they like?

They come from non-traditional backgrounds

In many countries around the world, institutions of higher education are seeing an influx of students from what are sometimes called 'non-traditional academic backgrounds': students whose parents did not themselves attain a high degree of education, and who come from homes where books are not in plentiful supply, or part of daily life, and whose routes to a place at university have been varied. According to statistics gathered by a UK government agency, in the 2006–2007 academic year 40% of 17–30 year olds in England participated in higher education (DIUS, 2008), and this trend is reflected in many countries where widening participation in higher education is a governmental objective. Today's universities are no longer populated by the elite, highly prepared few.

The risk for students from backgrounds where academic literacy was not emphasised is that they may arrive at university less prepared to manage a heavy reading load, find information in the library, and accommodate to the demands of academic writing, compared by Bourdieu and Passeron (1965) to writing in a foreign language. Pressures which cannot be managed by legitimate means may result in students feeling forced to find shortcuts and this may therefore be a partial cause of some cheating behaviours, including prototypical plagiarism. By the same token, weaknesses in both reading and writing skills are direct causes of patchwriting.

Conventions for academic writing and source use are part of a set of 'institutional practices of mystery' (Lillis, 2001), practices which serve in part as shibboleths to distinguish insiders from outsiders. Although such may not be their intent, these practices, which are often not made explicit, have been shown to cause students from non-traditional backgrounds to feel excluded (Lillis, 1997) or, more correctly to contribute to the effect of feeling excluded in which race, religion, age, social class, etc, can play a role.

Uncertainty about plagiarism in the face of the authority of the published text is a concern frequently articulated by students. A study of two UK universities found that

> students often expressed anxieties about plagiarism in terms of their own authority as writers. They were unclear about what actually constitutes plagiarism and yet at the same time were concerned about how to acknowledge the authority of academic texts. Their overriding concerns were that the texts they read were authoritative and that they as students had little useful to say.
>
> (Lea and Street, 1998: 167)

These concerns caused them to worry that they 'would plagiarise unknowingly', and these concerns are well founded particularly for students from diverse backgrounds. In an investigation set in South Africa, Angélil-Carter (2000) found that students with strong academic backgrounds were more confident about negotiating these boundaries, and that staff perceived their efforts as legitimate, while identifying the hesitant efforts of the non-traditional students as plagiarism. Given that plagiarism is a matter in which subjectivity and the need for interpretation already provide complications, broader diversity among students (for all the real and potential positives it offers) appears to create opportunities for further problems with plagiarism.

Angélil-Carter identifies another, more subtle but potentially more powerful issue, as well: authority. A good academic writer is a confident, authoritative one. To be able to construct a strong text, a writer first needs to have something to say. Having something to say presupposes knowing something and feeling confident enough about it to want to spread the word. Using sources effectively rests on a confident understanding of what they say and how they relate to the topic at hand. A problem that staff often identify in the work of inexperienced writers is the handing over of responsibility to the sources: texts become full of 'Smith says' and 'According to Jones', instead of the more varied, and more self-assured 'As Smith correctly notes' and 'While Smith maintains X, Jones strikes a contrasting note with Y'.

This authority is linked, for Angélil-Carter, with two other issues, language and role in society. Language ability relates to 'how the student projects herself or himself in tutorials, lectures and seminars' (2000: 130). However, connections between authority and language on the one hand, and students' backgrounds on the other, emerge:

> it is striking that most of the students struggling deeply with academic discourse that I interviewed were women from township or rural backgrounds. Also striking is that it was Nothando, a woman, and not Mangalisu, a man, who was *not* given the benefit of the doubt [by their examiner]. The women who were succeeding . . . were of privileged class and background. I do not wish readers to conclude from this that academic literacy problems relate only to certain groups of students . . . In any multiracial, gendered context, however, it may be that . . . authority is granted more easily to certain students, by those in positions of power, and withheld from others.
>
> (2000: 130)

Angélil-Carter is right to caution against assuming that the relationships between background and academic literacy are rigid and clear. However, it is clear that where language and authority matter, those who struggle to express themselves will be disadvantaged, as will those whose authority is threatened by being visibly different and thereby risking exclusion. (It is interesting to note in this connection that many of the issues identified in Chapter 7 to do with second-language users of English resonate with description as well.)

They're Millenials

The Millenials is the name sometimes given to the generational cohort which started reaching university in the early 2000s, also called Generation Y. One of the characteristics of this group is their constant plugged-in-ness. A Pew Research Center report on this generation was subtitled with three of their signal characteristics: 'Confident. Connected. Open to change', and calls the Millenials

> leading technology enthusiasts. For them, these innovations provide more than a bottomless source of information and entertainment, and more than a new ecosystem for their social lives. They also are a badge of generational identity. Many Millennials say their use of modern technology is what distinguishes them from other generations.
> (Taylor and Keeter, 2010: 25)

By every measure in the report, the Millenials' use of technology justifies this description. Compared to their predecessors they are more likely to hold positive attitudes toward technology, to use the Internet and, specifically to use social networking sites. They are also much more likely to connect to a wireless network with a laptop or handheld device when they are away from home or the office. Eighty-three per cent sleep with their cell phone close to hand, compared to 50% of Baby Boomers, and they send an average of 20 text messages a day, against GenX's 12.

The Millenials pursue higher education avidly. According to the same report, 63% either have finished or plan to finish a university degree. However, the current economic situation has been least kind to this generation, and the impact has been felt in part on their educational aspirations. Among those who are not actively working toward a degree or planning to, 'more than a third (36%) say that they can't afford [it] right now, and an additional 35% say they simply do not have the time' (Taylor and Keeter, 2010: 40). Time and money are not independent of each other, of course, and that affects those who are in higher education as well. Twenty-four per cent of Millenials combine study with work (as opposed to only 13% who study and do not work).

These three strands – time, money and a degree of connectedness such that for them media consumption is less about consuming media and more about being consumed – were factors Blum's (2010) study of US students and plagiarism identified as being implicated in the phenomenon. Blum explains that from an early age the students she and her team interviewed were engaged in a frantic schedule of extracurricular activities to make them more attractive candidates for a place at a competitive university, and, perhaps out of habit or out of a belief that the same image of being 'well rounded' will serve them in good stead when they look for employment, they continue a hectic round of activities once they get to university. Their lack of time means that 'they may dash off a paper, seeking mainly to satisfy requirements regarding number of pages, references, quotations' (2009: 4). Financial pressures cause them to work, and in the US context Blum studied, high tuition fees mean that students leave universities heavily in debt, and see their degrees as enabling them to get the jobs which will permit them to pay off the debt they have incurred. In this context plagiarism can be a by-product of a need to earn good grades in less than favourable circumstances.

Plagiarism can also be the result of a clash of generational cultures. Their connectedness has, Blum discovered,

> *changed* how they think of texts. They are engaged with media constantly. They spend hours watching TV, maybe whole series on DVD, or watching movies. And they quote from them to one another. This kind of quotation – one form of what academics call, so multisyllabically, *intertextuality* – shows verbal sophistication, memory, and sensitivity to context and appropriateness. This is very much what we ask them to do with academic texts, except that when they quote in an academic context, they have to slow way down, set up boundaries around each little piece of text, trace its origin, and document its source. This slowness and deliberateness is at odds with their customary focus on speed and efficiency.
>
> (2010: 4–5)

The Millenials are accustomed to using the Internet as a primary source of information, cutting and pasting content with great facility and little reflection, sharing links, pictures and videos on Facebook and retweeting contributions which deserve it, moving from medium to medium, device to device, activity to activity, and routinely using capabilities that translate voice to text and vice versa. For this generation, relating texts to each other in the way that academic writing traditionally prizes and requires is an alien and mysterious activity.

They are learning in different ways

Although the observation that the Internet has changed practices for teaching and learning is overworked, it cannot be avoided. Distance courses are growing in popularity, often offered by universities on the correct assumption that they can market a course more widely that way, and the incorrect assumption that distance teaching saves staff time and can therefore be offered more economically. They are popular with students, some of whom have living or family arrangements which make attendance in person impossible, and some of whom unrealistically conclude that while they do not have time to be physically present in class, they will be able to make the time for more self-directed study.

Campus-based courses feel the effects of new learning technologies as well. Learning platforms offer a new meeting place for students and teachers (and one where students may expect to be able to find their teachers 24 hours a day, seven days a week). In fields like the arts, where the number of teaching hours is traditionally small in comparison to the STEM subjects, the learning platform is expected to compensate for the much-needed contact hours which are not available. In class, transparencies have long been replaced by PowerPoint, which is in turn feeling its territory eroded by newer tools like Prezi, and increasingly the whiteboard is being replaced by smartboards, on which the lecturer's handwritten notes and prepared lecture slides can easily merge, and equally easily be uploaded later to the learning platform.

The factors which have been linked to prototypical plagiarism include a sense of detachment, from the educational system or the teacher, pressures of time and the sense that nobody is really hurt by it; in other words, balanced pressures on the one hand providing a reason to want (or perceive a need) to cheat, and on the other hand a justification for it. A distance learning environment means less direct contact between teachers and students, and among students; physical contact is certainly lost, and they may or may not speak directly to or see each other. That may provide the sense that the impact of cheating is less personal, and therefore more justifiable.

Difficulty in understanding the boundaries between someone else's ideas and one's own has been seen to be a contributing factor to patchwriting, and it is thought that hypertext and electronic media may exacerbate this effect (Belcher, 2001). As more course content exists on servers and in clouds, rather than between the covers of a book, the challenges students face in reconciling their notions of authorship and due acknowledgement with those of their teachers will not grow easier.

Implications for teaching about plagiarism and source use

The changes to the composition of the student body mean that if it was ever safe to make assumptions about who students are, what their abilities are when they start university, and how they position themselves in relation to teachers, fellow students, libraries, textbooks and all else that is part of the university experience, it no longer is. Many of these changes have the effect of making a traditional approach to teaching about plagiarism and source use a poor fit. This is not necessarily a bad thing.

As earlier chapters have shown, our attitudes toward plagiarism and source use need revisiting. Academics do not agree with each other about what plagiarism is, but have hitherto shown an unacademic lack of interest in problematising our differences. We define it in general terms and categorise it as an appropriation but identify it in our students' work by means of a quantitative measure of how similarly two texts are worded, produced by a machine which is unable to gauge originality in any other terms. We decry plagiarism as an offence which threatens the fabric of academic values but, as the next chapter will show, we engage in intertextual practices which run equally counter to academic values, and which we would not allow in the work of our students.

Translating our expectations for a diverse group of students, some of whom have come from environments which do not prize the text and its unitary author the way academics do, some of whom we will only interact with via a learning platform, and some of whom are firmly entrenched in the very different literacy practices of the connected generation will take creativity. It will also require us to think more clearly than we are often wont to do about what aspects of plagiarism offend, and why. And that will be a salutary experience. Thinking clearly, challenging assumptions, basing conclusions on evidence rather than accepted practice is what academics do – isn't it?

Activity

Understanding diversity. This chapter made reference to 'institutional practices of mystery', one of which is the set of rules and conventions for citation and source use. The purpose of this activity is to learn about which practices are mysterious to students. Interview a student (not one of your own) and ask the student to:

- describe a recent piece of assessed course work. What did the assignment call for?
- explain what the student believes the examiner was looking for. What was necessary for success on the assignment? What would cause it to receive a low grade?
- explain whether completing the assignment involved reading and/or referring to sources. If so, which ones?
- describe what rules the student was expected to follow in using those sources. How did the student learn those rules?

Questions for discussion or reflection

1 Think about your own time as a student. What was a typical week like? How many hours did you spend in class, and how many studying outside of class? What study materials did you use (i.e., notes from lectures, lecturers' slides, library materials, etc.)? Did you work, and if so how much? What free-time

activities did you have, and how much time did you spend on them? How do your experiences compare to those of your students?

2 A characteristic attributed by Blum (2009) to the students she studied is that they are collaborative. How would you explain to a student where the boundary lies between appropriate forms of collaboration and collusion.

3 On distance courses teachers may assess the work of students they have never met in person, or possibly never spoken to or seen via webcam. Do those circumstances have any implications for the way you usually work with plagiarism and source use?

4 The idea was introduced earlier in this chapter that students who have grown up as part of a culture of connectedness perceive intertextual boundaries differently. Consider this contradictory idea from an essay on plagiarism as theft:

> My students *do know* that plagiarism is regarded as transgressive by the academic community; they also *know* a great deal about the details of academic norms – that paraphrase and websites need citation, that quotes must be exact, that even ideas must be referenced; they *know* that the dominant model for plagiarism is not cooperation of transitional textuality, but *theft*. But for all they do know, many of them *don't believe* . . . Students routinely download files and music illegally, and they don't have much compunction about it.
>
> (Senders, 2008: 196)

Which of these perspectives – that students understand plagiarism differently from their teachers, or that they understand it the way their teachers do but don't care – is closer to the reality for your students? If Senders' description seems realistic to you, what is the source of the not caring?

10

Plagiarism in a broader context

Summary

This chapter considers source use in domains other than academic writing. It explores whether universities themselves apply the policies they require their students to follow. An analysis of the recursive example of university plagiarism policies demonstrates clear inconsistencies. The impact of this inconsistency on students struggling to know when and how to apply the policies is considered. The need to have practical plagiarism policies leads to the topic of common knowledge, which is used to illustrate the ways that conventions and principles for source use grow out of dynamic intertextual relationships.

Source use practices in academia are steeped in centuries of convention but are not those used in all domains. Source use in workplace genres is used as an illustration for the often poor fit between what students are taught to do at university and what they need to do in the workplace. That gap is not problematic if the genres are different but the skills are transferable. However, an approach to source use which casts rules as static also casts genres and writing skills more generally that way, reducing the likelihood that students learn writing skills which they can translate to other domains.

When you have finished this chapter you will be aware of inconsistencies in the way academic understandings of, and practices with regard to source use relate to the standards to which students are held. You will understand the resulting challenge that this entails for students, and be able to address this more effectively in your teaching.

Plagiarism has been shown to relate to a number of issues related to teaching, learning, writing, and orientations toward knowledge creation. The quotation below discusses one such related issue, the question of what counts as 'common knowledge', and the discussion later in this chapter develops the issue further. What other concepts related to plagiarism deserve exploration in a broader context?

> By framing conversations and instruction about common knowledge in the larger context of discourse community conventions and expectations, we can help our students move beyond the formulaic handbook approach to resolve questions on common knowledge in several ways. They will be able to approach common knowledge and citation practices from a more informed perspective, one that takes into account the effect of their audience on how and what they cite . . . resolving questions about the dynamics of common knowledge can promote critical thinking, discussion, and reflection about the larger issues of source citation and intertextuality. In short, we can help students develop the qualities of academic thinkers and writers we set as goals for our classes.
>
> (England, 2008: 112)

So far this volume has treated plagiarism as a phenomenon which impinges upon the processes of teaching, learning and assessment at university. Plagiarism has also been approached from the assumption that it is a problematic phenomenon, and one which must be prevented. Prototypical plagiarism is problematic for all the reasons that any form of cheating is. Reasons to be concerned about patchwriting include the fact that it can cause students to incur precisely the same penalties as for deceptive plagiarism. The book has also argued that since the cause of much plagiarism lies in the limitations in students' skills in writing from sources, a pedagogical solution is called for.

This chapter, however, looks beyond the domain of student assessment writing to examine source use in other contexts. It shows that the standards and practices for source use which apply to student writing are not universal, and that too myopic a view on plagiarism in that domain may have negative consequences for what students understand about writing within and outside of the university.

Practicing what we preach?

The definition of plagiarism in Example 10.1 below appeared in Chapter 1. It was taken from the website of a university in the UK which will be referred to here as University Alpha[v], and is part of the University Calendar (i.e. regulations). The definition appears at the bottom of the page as an Appendix to the regulations on academic integrity. A copyright notice appears at the bottom, but there is no information about the authorship of the material on the page. This is not surprising in that regulations and policies rarely identify their authorship, and are in fact presumably most often the result of a collaborative writing process in which many people were involved in different ways. However, it is noteworthy because a student who wanted to cite the regulations for any reason would find that the quick-reference examples given in 'how not to plagiarise' instructions, which are typically to books or journal articles or other materials with an identified author, would not provide a good model. This is of course not an insuperable obstacle, but it is an example of how the instructions for avoiding plagiarism given to students do not always correspond to intertextual realities.

Example 10.1

Academic Integrity Statement: Appendix 1

Plagiarism is the reproduction or paraphrasing, without acknowledgement, from **public or private (ie: unpublished)** material (including material downloaded from the Internet) attributable to, or which is the intellectual property of, another including the work of students.

Plagiarism may be of written and also non-written form and therefore would also include the unacknowledged use of computer programs, mathematical/ computer models/algorithms, computer software in all forms, macros, spreadsheets, web pages, databases, mathematical deviations and calculations, designs/models/displays of any sort, diagrams, graphs, tables, drawings, works of art of any sort, fine art pieces or artefacts, digital images, computer-aided design drawings, GIS files, photographs, maps, music/ composition of any sort, posters, presentations and tracing.**

** (this is not an exhaustive list).

Further up on the page is a list of bullet points answering the question 'What is academic integrity and why is it important?' One point offered is that it includes 'fully acknowledging the work of others wherever it has contributed to your own (thereby avoiding plagiarism [see Appendix 1])'. In this spirit of following the principles articulated in the definition and other parts of the policy there is an attribution to University Beta.

This is clearly a point on which academic institutions are in agreement, because it is also made in the same words, but without the reference to Appendix 1, in the 'Academic integrity regulations' of University Gamma, also in the UK (Example 10.2). Large portions of that policy are identical to the source of 10.1, or virtually so. For example, 'software' has been moved up the list of things which are 'plagiarisable' and the note from University Alpha that 'this is not an exhaustive list' now reads 'this list is not exhaustive'. However, University Gamma does not attribute any part of the policy to any source. Neither does University Delta, located in China – See Example 10.3 for an extract from its 'Regulations for MSc and PhD students', nor Institution Epsilon, a further education college located in London and the source of Example 10.4.

Example 10.2

3.1 **Plagiarism** is the reproduction or paraphrasing, without acknowledgement, from **public or private (ie: unpublished)** material (including material downloaded from the Internet) attributable to, or which is the intellectual property of, another including the work of students.

3.2 Plagiarism may be of written and also non-written form and therefore would also include the unacknowledged use of computer programs or software, mathematical/computer models/algorithms, macros, spreadsheets, web pages, databases, designs/models/displays of any sort, diagrams, graphs, tables, drawings, works of art of any sort, digital images, computer-aided design drawings, GIS files, photographs, maps, music/composition of any sort, posters, presentations and tracing. This list is not exhaustive.

Example 10.3

Plagiarism is the reproduction or paraphrasing, without acknowledgement, from *public or private (ie: unpublished)* material (including material downloaded from the Internet) attributable to, or which is the intellectual property of, another including the work of students.

Plagiarism may be of written and also non-written form and therefore would also include the unacknowledged use of computer programs, mathematical/computer models/algorithms, computer software in all forms, macros, spreadsheets, web pages, databases, mathematical derivations and calculations, designs/models/displays of any sort, diagrams, charts, graphs, tables, drawings, works of art of any sort, fine art pieces or artefacts, digital images, computer aided design drawings, GIS files, photographs, maps, music/composition of any sort, posters, presentations, *etc.*

Example 10.4

Plagiarism is the reproduction or paraphrasing, without acknowledgement, from public or private (i.e.: unpublished) material (including material downloaded from the Internet) attributable to, or which is the intellectual property of, another including the work of students. This is a serious offence, with severe penalties. You will be given information on plagiarism when you begin your studies, and can speak to your personal tutor at any time.

The point of these examples is not to suggest that these universities engaged in bad practice (and most certainly not University Alpha, which identified its source). It would be for the author or authors of the original document to say whether they feel they deserved acknowledgement. However, it is manifestly the case that Institutions Beta, Gamma, Delta and Epsilon are guilty of not practicing what they preach. And while there is considerable irony in copying and pasting off the Internet a policy which says students must not do precisely that, the inconsistency of the message is possibly a source of greater concern.

These are not isolated cases; many more examples of 'policy recycling' from many other universities can be found. Policies are precisely the sort of documents which are treated as 'boilerplate' and copied, with or without adjustments, from one context to another. Nor is recycling wrong (although whether or not it is done with permission of the author is relevant). There is no reason to re-invent the wheel, and every reason not to: consistency across universities would be to everybody's advantage.

The problem lies in the message that this inconsistent behaviour sends. Students struggle to make sense of conventions and rules which are entirely or partially new to them when they arrive in an academic setting. They frequently perceive those rules as being arcane (Bloch, 2012) and less clear than the straightforward assertions of many policies would suggest. They are also digitally literate, and turn to Google for information more readily than to the university library. It will not escape them that the message they are getting is 'do as I say, not as I do'. The interesting lesson which universities can learn from, if they choose, is that the reality of how we use and attribute sources is considerably more complex than that which we present to students when we tell them that we expect them to avoid plagiarism.

Preach something practicable

One piece of information frequently offered to students is that references are not needed when the idea in question is common knowledge. What does this mean in practice? This is another area in which that which students are told is inadequate, and therefore extremely unhelpful. The website of a US university has a page headed 'Plagiarism prevention for students' (perhaps to distinguish the advice offered there from the rules which apply to policy makers, who have been seen to consider themselves licensed to copy and paste from the Internet without attributing their sources). The page on common knowledge begins like this:

Example 10.5

There is no clear boundary on what is considered common knowledge. Even experts on plagiarism disagree on what counts as common knowledge. For instance, many sources only consider facts – current and historical events, famous people, geographic areas, etc. – to be potentially common knowledge. Others also include nonfactual material such as folklore and common sayings. Some sources limit common knowledge to only information known by others in your class, other sources look at what is common knowledge for the broader subject area.

A student who had been paying attention to the admonition to attribute the source of information would at this point ask 'Which experts on plagiarism? Which sources?' The discussion continues to offer more unsupported assertions, and also to reveal that the writer does not know the singular form of 'criteria':

Example 10.5 (contd)

The two criteria that are most commonly used in deciding whether or not something is common knowledge relate to quantity: the fact can be found in numerous places and ubiquity: it is likely to be known by a lot of people. Ideally both conditions are true. A third criteria [*sic*] that is sometimes used is whether the information can be easily found in a general reference source.

Example 10.6

As a general rule, a fact can be said to be 'common knowledge' when:

- it is widely accessible – you may not know the total population of China, but you would be able to find the answer easily from numerous sources

- it is likely to be known by a lot of people
- it can be found in a general reference resource, such as a dictionary or encyclopedia

Example 10.6 is from a UK university. According to this 'general rule', common knowledge is something which may come from a source but which, if retold without a citation to the source, exposes the writer to minimal chances of detection, because it could have been found in many places. Also according to this principle, I do not need to provide a citation for the fact that the derisory American term 'doofus' may derive from the Scots word *doof*, meaning 'dolt', because the source of this fact – unknown to me until a minute ago – is the *Oxford English Dictionary*, surely the definitive general reference resource. Another source, a US university, gives the examples of common knowledge in 10.7:

Example 10.7
___

Examples of common knowledge are:

- There are four seasons in the year.
- There are 365 days in a year.
- The US entered World War II after the bombing of Pearl Harbor.
- The state bird of Georgia is the brown thrasher.

The difficulty with these examples is that it is hard to imagine a context in which this advice could be used. It would be surprising if there were many university research papers which have based their argument on the idea that there are four seasons, or 365 days, in the year, but more surprising still if their writers needed advice about whether to provide a citation for the fact. It is perhaps only slightly easier to imagine an academic writing context in which naming the state bird of Georgia would be relevant, but if I found myself in such a circumstance I believe I would want to provide a citation. It is not a fact I know, so I would need to consult a source, and having consulted it, would want to cite it.

Another university from the US offers this final explanation:

Example 10.8
___

Common knowledge needs no internal citation in a paper. Common knowledge includes information that is considered a well-established fact verifiable in five or more sources.

This explanation founders on all the previous difficulties: the fact that it can be found in multiple places does not mean it is widely known. In addition, it offers the false promise of a definite rule which is in fact not reliable. Google offers nearly 200,000 sites which either explain or exemplify the meaning of the term 'fabric-based infrastructure' but it is not part of my understanding of common knowledge. If it is yours, you may find an alternative explanation of common knowledge more appealing.

I offer this alternative not because I wish to argue for the fact that this should be the accepted definition (although I believe it has merit) but to illustrate two points about source use: first, that the question of common knowledge (and by extension other questions about source use) can be resolved more effectively by returning to first principles than by articulating mechanical rules; and secondly, that there are explanations to be had which are grounded in critical analysis, and therefore ought to be what students are offered, by way of modelling good academic practices, rather than uncritically accepted and parroted truisms of questionable truth.

This alternative explanation draws on three ideas: 1) transparent source use, i.e., the principle that the reader should be able to deduce how sources have been used; 2) an informed understanding of what 'common' means or can mean in a context related to communication; and 3) the assumption that avoiding plagiarism is not the only, nor even the primary, purpose of citation.

The principle of transparent source use says that the reader should be able to understand which sources have materially influenced a new text, and how. From this perspective, I would certainly need to provide a citation for the origins of 'dufus' and the meaning of 'fabric-based infrastructure', because I can trace my knowledge of them back to specific sources. If citation is in part about acknowledging an intellectual debt, as the definitions above suggest, then I owe that debt to my sources, and it is not relevant how many other sources *could* have informed me, any more than it is relevant that, when I left my wallet at home, I could have borrowed money for a sandwich from any one of a number of colleagues – it is the one who actually lent me the money who wants repaying.

Another understanding of common knowledge comes from reflecting on the word 'common', which has a sense which means something like 'found everywhere' but also has the sense of 'shared'. This suggests that common knowledge is shared knowledge, and in the case of ideas which do or do not need references, it is presumably the writer and the (intended) reader who should share them. When I lecture on clause structure and tell students that the word 'red' in the sentence *Jeff painted the house red* is an object predicative, I do not provide a reference. They have read the textbook (or at least we maintain a polite pretence that they have). So have I. We have a common source of information. In other words, we have knowledge which is common among us.

Finally, the most relevant point might not be whether a citation is needed, but whether it is helpful. In identifying 'red' an object predicative above, I have asserted a fact which I believe to be common knowledge by my first definition but not my second. It is a piece of knowledge about my subject which I have had so long that identifying the source from which I first learned it would be impossible. I suspect that some but not all readers of this book know what an object predicative is, so in that sense it is not knowledge that is common to those of us having this conversation. However, I also assume that if you have ever heard of an object predicative, you know why 'red' is one in that sentence, and if you have not, you probably do not care: you understand it to be of importance only to illustrate the point, namely that whether subject-specific terminology is common knowledge depends entirely on the audience with whom it is used. If I am right in my predictions, then omitting a citation is considerate to both sets of readers.

However, in the last chapter, in connection with claims about students and electronic media, I referenced Joel Bloch's and Susan Blum's informative books on the topic. The claims for which I cited them are quite uncontroversial in my professional literature. They do not particularly need support, nor do I feel an intellectual debt in the sense that these are ideas which are 'in the air' – I did not necessarily learn them from these authors, although they have contributed to my understanding of the topic. However, I assume that a reader who has come this far in a book about teaching to avoid plagiarism may be interested in reading either or both of those important books, and the citations are intended as a helpful act to that reader, more than out of a sense of obligation on my part.

To conclude, I propose that common knowledge can be understood by interpreting it to mean 'shared' and 'already known', and when it is both no citation is needed, although a reader may find one useful. The 'already known' criterion – the one relating to transparency – is one about which only the writer can speak, based on reflection on what sources have informed his or her understanding of a topic. The other two criteria, what information the reader shares with the writer, and what information the reader needs, are more tenuous still. They are based on a prediction the writer makes about a reader who may be known (e.g., the teacher) or may be only imagined. Asking students to engage in acts of mind reading and prediction may seem like setting the bar for them rather high, but anticipating the reader's needs is part of all good writing. Given a choice between asking my students to take on the difficult piece of analysis which is anticipating the reactions of the expected reader, or making decisions about their writing based on highly hedged, unrealistic and mechanical rules of thumb, I will choose the former, as being more consistent with the intellectual engagement which ought to characterise a university education.

Getting real

In many educational contexts, and in many subject areas, an important purpose of a university education is to prepare the student for their later role in the workplace. One means of doing this is by providing transferable outcomes: learning outcomes realised during the years of a university education which can be applied to new domains once the student reaches the workplace. However, as has been frequently noted (e.g., Dias *et al.*, 2000), the sort of assessment writing students do at university offers too little in the way of transferable outcomes; the sort of writing done in the workplace is very different from the academic essay, and even different in important respects from assessment genres which attempt to simulate workplace genres, such as the case study or report.

Many of the differences which can be noted are related to intertextual practices, and the ways which sources (either earlier texts or collaborating co-authors) are involved in the writing process. Students are exhorted to conceive of the writing task as a forum for putting forward an original idea, to use sources to provide credible support for that idea, to cite the sources they use, and to do their own work. The ability to do these things, which has already been shown to be so difficult for students to cultivate, is not always required by or prized in workplace genres. A study of the writing which Canadian students did at university and on internships (Schneider and Andre, 2005), found that in one of the three subject areas studied, students had engaged in collaborative writing at university, and this served them well in the workplace, where it was expected of them, while students from other subject areas had not had this experience, but could have benefitted from it.

There is clear evidence that many 'real-world' genres make heavy use of sources without attributing their influences as clearly as is expected in academic writing, or indeed even at all. Solin (2004) examined journalistic writing, looking at the treatment given the same topic by different outlets. She used the metaphor of recycling to describe the sorts of text re-use she found, which occurred either without attribution or with, she concluded, the wrong attribution. However, and quite importantly, it was not a plagiarism free-for-all; the text recycling occurred in certain functional sections of articles but not others. This suggests that the writers are behaving in a rule-based manner, that they perceive themselves as following conventions which permit some types of recycling but not others.

An important business genre is the corporate annual report, and within it, the 'Chairman's Statement' which occupies an early and prominent position. The annual report is tightly circumscribed by regulation, both in the fact of having to produce one and the sort of information which must be provided in it. The Chairman's Statement is used to provide a gloss to the facts and figures in the report, putting forth the interpretation which the company itself hopes will be placed upon them. The practices of this very important genre in using and referring to sources bears little relation to the practices of academic writing, the practices which are taught to students, some of whom will one day have to produce this genre (Shaw and Pecorari, 2013).

Chairman's Statements make many claims, but rarely support them with reference to a source. When they do, the reference may echo the sort of information given in a citation in an academic work, but is naturally qualitatively quite different. Examples 10.9 and 10.10 illustrate this; they refer to a source text ('my half year statement' and 'my report last year'), the 'author' (in each case the 'I' who will sign the Chairman's Statement, and takes formal responsibility for the documents referred to, but would have been extremely unlikely actually to have authored either of them); and by inference the date of publication of the source can be retrieved (the same year in 10.9 and the previous year in 10.10).

In this genre, references to source thus appear in a very different form than in academic writing, when they appear at all; more common still, though, is the unsupported assertion of a fact, as in Example 10.11. Assertions of the sort there would, if produced in a piece of academic writing, require a reference to an authoritative source.

Example 10.9

In my half year statement I reported that [name] had retired from the Board on 18 April.

Example 10.10

In my report last year I detailed our plan for restoring the fortunes of [company].

Example 10.11

The expansion of illicit trade is a continuing and growing threat to the business. Sharp increases in excise duty, pressure on consumers' disposable income, and ill-considered regulation of our industry, are all making life easier and more lucrative for traders of illicit products, both contraband and counterfeit.

Similarly, the writers of these texts sometimes use a 'template' or 'boilerplate' approach to producing them, with the previous year's text taken as the starting point for producing the new one. This may result in sections of one year's statement being reproduced in identical form the next year, as in Example 10.12, or in modest changes to update the factual content which has changed from one year to the next, as in Example 10.13. This approach to production is in stark contrast to the demands for originality placed on academic writers, and additionally suggests that the ownership of the text does not rest with the individual or individuals who produced it.

Example 10.12

From the 2008 report

Once again I have been extremely impressed by the commitment and professionalism of all our employees, especially in this challenging economic environment.

From the 2009 report

Once again I have been extremely impressed by the commitment and professionalism of all our employees, especially in this challenging economic environment.

Example 10.13

From the 2007 report

The Board is recommending a final dividend of 5.02 pence per ordinary share which, when added to the interim dividend of 3.04 pence, gives a total for the year of 8.06 pence, a 20.0% increase on 2006.

From the 2008 report

The Board is recommending a final dividend of 6.28 pence per ordinary share which, when added to the interim dividend of 3.80 pence, gives a total for the year of 10.08 pence, a 25.0% increase on 2007.

Example 10.14

From the 2000 report

As a company Aggreko is totally committed to enhancing shareholder value by delivering consistent growth in quality earnings through an ever expanding range of added value services focused on solving customers increasingly complex temporary power temperature control and oil free compressed air requirements around the world.

From the 2001 report

As a company Aggreko is committed to enhancing shareholder value by delivering growth in quality earnings through an ever expanding range of added value services focused on solving customers increasingly complex temporary power temperature control and oil free compressed air requirements around the world.

The normal, conventional, accepted practices of writers in the workplace are therefore very sharply at odds with the practices which are urged upon academic writers, and sources are used (or not used) in a range of 'real-world' genres in ways which would cause academic writers to be criticised. There is a fundamental clash in what is expected in these two domains which limits the transferability of what is taught about writing, and source use, at university.

A paper on collusion in university assessed work begins by observing that 'an increasing emphasis on developing students' transferable skills, such as group working and IT, is creating challenges in ensuring the academic integrity of individually assessed coursework' (Sutton and Taylor, 2011: 831). An alternative perspective would be that a heavy emphasis on academic integrity, and on preventing plagiarism, and on promoting academic ideals for source use, is creating challenges in ensuring the transferability of students' learning at university to the workplace.

It should be noted that the fact that academic genres are not the same as workplace genres need not preclude the possibility of transferability from one to the other. Indeed, one of the often stated advantages of an education in the humanities is that it equips the student with the skills of reading, writing and above all critical thinking which are foundational in most enterprises. The ability to address a given type of reader effectively should itself be a transferable outcome, and confer, or at least help to develop, the ability to address a different kind of reader next time.

The difficulty is that that presupposes an instructional model which promotes the lateral thinking which remapping one set of writing skills onto a new domain requires. As Hunt (n.d.) notes,

> a model which assumes that a skill like 'writing the academic essay' is an ability which can be demonstrated on demand, quite apart from any authentic rhetorical situation, actual question, or expectation of effect (or definition of what the 'academic essay' actually *is*), virtually prohibits students from recognizing that all writing is shaped by rhetorical context and situation, and thus renders them tone-deaf to the shifts in register and diction which make so much plagiarized undergraduate text instantly recognizable.

By the same token, teaching a set of mechanical rules for source use (you do *not* need to provide a reference for the state bird of Georgia) discourages students from thinking about the sorts of things which they would need to think about if, instead of believing in rules for source use, they asked questions. Finding answers to questions about what should be cited, when, and how involves a sensitivity to readership, textual purpose, genre and the like, and it is that sensitivity which permits writers to transfer their skills from one domain to another.

Conclusion

This chapter has set the question of plagiarism in student writing within the context of practices inside and outside the university. The source-use practices in two domains have been profiled: plagiarism policies and the writing of people outside the university. In addition, practices for understanding when to cite or not have been examined indirectly through the advice given to students. This analysis has revealed that the success or failure of an approach can only be judged in context.

The use of more references, and to more authoritative, external sources would not improve the effectiveness of a Chairman's Statement; in fact, a greater reliance on citation would limit the ability to make the sort of claims which the writers feel it important to make. The advice given to students about common knowledge is, I have argued, often deeply flawed, but not because it runs counter to a set of externally validated rules; it is flawed because it does not reflect the reality of how students use sources. It is not within the scope of this book to comment on the ethics of copying an academic integrity policy without attributing its source, but the fact of having done so must almost certainly affect the credibility with which students will read it, so this use of sources too is flawed because it is ineffective.

It is ultimately the lack of a connection to the realities of writing and the context in which it happens which is problematic, not only in these examples but more generally. An approach to plagiarism which emphasises simple and clear-cut rules and casts plagiarism as primarily a matter of ethical questions with clear boundaries is destined to fall short of its mark. An approach which understands plagiarism as a particular relationship between the writer, the reader, the new text and its sources, treats learning about that relationship as a developmental process, and emphasises teaching good skills over punishing poor performance will be much more realistic, and will have better chances of success.

Activity

Transitioning from university to workplace. Think about the sort of workplace your students may typically wind up in when they finish university. Make a list of the sorts of writing they will need to do in that environment.

- What sort of role does reading and reference to sources play in producing those texts?
- How will the expectations for good source use, writing and acknowledgement be similar or different? For example, will they be expected to write

collaboratively? Will they be credited as authors on the documents they produce? Will they typically be expected to append a reference list to the texts they write?

Now reflect on the sorts of writing your students do at university.

- Do they write the genres which they are likely to produce later in the workplace?
- What proficiencies do their writing assignments cultivate?
- What target audience(s) do they address? Is there a need to be able to adapt to different audiences?
- What purposes do they have for doing written work (apart from passing the course)?
- What issues to do with style and register arise in your students' assessment work?

Questions for discussion or reflection

1 Are there writing tasks to which you would find it acceptable to bring a 'template' or 'boilerplate' approach? What are they? In what sorts of writing is that approach not acceptable?

2 This chapter suggested a way to understand what common knowledge is, in order to understand what sort of ideas do not need to be referenced. What if anything might be added to or altered in this interpretation?

3 Some types of texts, such as the policy documents discussed in the first part of this chapter, often appear without their authorship identified. Does that reduce the need for a writer who uses ideas from them to include an attribution to them?

4 In a rich analysis of the difficulties involved in writing policies for plagiarism which leave scope for pedagogy, Price (2002) identifies one of the problematic aspects as the idea of 'one's "own" work', which figures prominently in the policies she studies, and indeed in many, if not most. Among the awkward and hard-to-make-sense-of ideas she identifies are the fact that the notion of the unitary author who creates new and original works 'from scratch' is a modern one, and collaborative learning, which is built on eroding the boundaries around 'one's "own" work'.

Is distinguishing what is one's own work problematic for you with regard to your students' writing? Do they have difficulties with the idea? Are there pedagogical practices which are effective for learning but approach the boundaries of collusion? Do you collaborate with colleagues in your professional life in ways which could require the boundaries of 'one's own' to be considered?

Appendix A   Training teachers in a good source-use pedagogy

This appendix describes a possible layout for a staff training seminar on teaching to promote good source use and avoid plagiarism. It is planned to take three one-hour sessions which can be offered back to back or distributed over a longer period, and requires no preparation on the part of participants (apart for an optional variation in the third session). However, because the content of each hour is based on key concepts presented earlier in this book, there are opportunities to coordinate reading portions of the book with the seminar sessions, either beforehand as preparation or afterwards by way of reinforcing and deepening. It presupposes a general in-service audience (i.e., participants from across the curriculum and at various teaching ranks) and no prior knowledge of the topic, but with some teaching experience.

Part I   What is plagiarism?

This introductory session is designed to take approximately the first hour of the seminar and introduces key concepts in the topic.

A   Prepare examples of possible plagiarism to distribute to participants, possibly Examples 1.7–1.9 from Chapter 1. Ask participants to decide whether they are acceptable ways to use sources or not, and if not, whether or not they are plagiarism. If participants find it hard to decide about one or more examples, ask them to express the reasons for their uncertainty and/ or what additional information they would want to make a decision.

B   Defining plagiarism. Compare a definition of plagiarism in use at your university, from as authoritative a source as possible, with others, for example, the ones in Chapter 1, or ones taken from other institutions which offer a relevant point of comparison or contrast to yours. Do the definitions help shed light on whether the examples in (A) were plagiarised? Introduce the four criteria for plagiarism (Chapter 1) and ask participants to analyse the definitions for explicit or implicit reference to them. Then return to the examples used in (A). Which of the four criteria are, or appear to be, at work there?

Part II How do we handle plagiarism?

This session should equip staff with a good working knowledge of the rules and procedures in place at their institution. This being the case, the content will vary from university to university, but by the end of this second hour they should have answers to the following questions.

- What rules (if any) state what students should be told about plagiarism at the start of a class?
- What steps does the university take to inform students about plagiarism? What information are they given, and where and how is it made available to them?
- What information is given to students about how to use sources appropriately?
- Does the university provide a subscription to a text-comparison service? Is its use by staff optional or mandatory? May students choose not to have their work submitted to it, or are they required to agree to that? What training in using and interpreting its results is available?
- What (if anything) do the regulations of this university require teachers to do about suspected plagiarism? What are the penalties for not doing it?
- What discretion do teachers have for deciding what action to take?
- What happens if a formal accusation of plagiarism is made against a student? What are the procedures and the possible penalties?

Part III A positive plagiarism pedagogy

Start by presenting the following key features of effective teaching for good source use (Chapter 5 elaborates on these), pausing after each for discussion about how this already happens in participants' courses, or how courses can be adjusted so that it does happen.

- Students should have clear targets, in terms of both what they are expected to do, and what they are *not* expected to do.
- These should ideally be expressed as anticipated learning outcomes, so that student performance in reaching the targets can be taken into account in the overall assessment.
- Expectations for source-use skills should be reasonable; students should be able to meet them with the skills and knowledge they can reasonably be expected to bring with them, and/or what they will be taught about writing and source use during the course.

- Assignments should be designed to encourage original responses and to permit good feedback.
- Feedback should explicitly address successful and unsuccessful source use, which requires the evaluator to *know*, not guess, how sources have been used.
- Opportunities for revision will permit students to refine their skills.

Variation: this session can be run effectively workshop-style, with participants coming prepared with an assignment they give their students and possibly examples of student responses to it. An outcome of the workshop can be to adjust the assignment and related procedures to ensure a better and more consistent outcome with regard to source use.

Appendix B   Case studies

These case studies are intended to be largely free-standing from the rest of the book, in the sense that they can be read and worked through in any order. However, Case 1 makes a particularly good companion to Chapters 1–2; Case 2 to Chapters 2–3; Case 3 to Chapter 3; Case 4 to Chapters 4–5; and Case 5 to Chapters 7, 9 and 10. One productive way to use Cases 6 and 7 is to work with them near the beginning of the book, revisit them near the middle and return to them at the end, to see if your impressions change.

The cases are in addition designed to accommodate different purposes, interests and time constraints. The first four cases describe a series of events around plagiarism in some detail. The fifth describes a set of attitudes to plagiarism and is considerably less detailed. It thus lends itself to use in contexts where only a modest amount of time is available for working with or discussing the case. The final two are based on student texts as well as interviews with the students and their supervisors. They are designed to support a deep, fine-grained analysis and a fact-based discussion.

Case 1: Disputed responsibility

In 2004, plagiarism from the Internet was discovered in the work of a student at a UK university pursuing a BA in English Literature. The student was near the end of his degree course, and after the plagiarism was identified in one of his later pieces of work, his earlier work was also reviewed. The same strategy of interweaving material copied and pasted into written assignments had been used throughout. A decision was made within the university to award no marks at all to his assessed work, making it impossible for him to receive his degree.

In the wide press coverage which attended this case, the student made the following points:

- He did not dispute the university's characterisation of his work, and agreed that he had used a cutting-and-pasting strategy throughout his degree.
- He stated that he had not been aware, until it was pointed out to him, that this strategy violated the rules. Having had the rules drawn to his attention, he agreed it did.

- He said that the university had a responsibility to tell him earlier in his course of study that his use of sources was inappropriate; waiting until the end of a three-year course to provide that feedback was unacceptable.
- He made reference to the fact that he had incurred £11,000 of debt during his studies, an investment of time and money which was now seen to be fruitless.

The Deputy Vice Chancellor of the university was quoted in the *Times Higher Education Supplement* this way:

> I would stress that the university has robust and well-established procedures in place to combat plagiarism and that our students are given clear guidance on this issue . . . in the faculty and department handbooks. Departments also supplement the formal documents with detailed advice and guidance to students.

The university's current documentation at time of writing, eight years after the case, includes a web page headed 'What is plagiarism?' ((1), below) with definitions very much like those seen in Chapters 1 and 10. It is approximately 200 words in length and concludes with the advice that 'What constitutes plagiarism for different subject areas may vary', and refers students to links on three faculty web pages.

The link for the Faculty of Humanities, where the student in question was presumably enroled, leads to a page headed 'Information for new research students' (2); (the student in question was an undergraduate). That page is approximately four screens long, with plagiarism appearing at the very bottom. The information on plagiarism there is a paraphrased version of the information in (1), concluding with a link to a page on academic integrity. That page says nothing specific about plagiarism but links to a page headed 'How do I avoid plagiarism?' (3).

That page, just under 200 words in length, includes statements like 'plagiarism can best be avoided by following good academic practice, which invoves correct academic referencing'. Following the links on this page leads to examples and definitions of quotation and paraphrase, among other things.

Links to the university web pages:

(1) http://www.kent.ac.uk/ai/students/whatisplagiarism.html
(2) http://www.kent.ac.uk/humanities/postgraduate/infopg.html#Plagiarism
(3) http://www.kent.ac.uk/ai/students/avoidingplagiarism.html

Read more about the case from these accounts:

Baty, P. (2004), 'Plagiarist student to sue university'. *The Times Online*. Retrieved January 19, 2006, from http://www.timesonline.co.uk/article/0,,3561-1126250,00.html.

Guardian Unlimited (2004, 24 May) 'Plagiarising student sues university for negligence'. Retrieved 18 January 2007 from http://education.guardian.co.uk/print/0,,4934062-108229,00.html.

Discussion

The disagreement in this case centred around responsibility: was it the student's responsibility to know the rules and therefore know that he was breaking them, or the university's responsibility to inform the student that the rules had been broken. Discuss that question from these perspectives:

- To what extent can a student be expected to take responsibility for applying a general rule to his or her coursework?
- Does the financial debt the student incurred alter your evaluation of the situation?
- What should or could the student and/or the university have done differently to avoid this outcome?
- Given that events unfolded as they did, what solutions might be found for this situation?

Case 2: Economies of scale

A master's student in engineering at a university in the US midwest was applying for a PhD studentship, and to understand how he might write a more effective proposal, began reading completed theses and dissertations, as well as some of their sources. He discovered that many of them repeated language from their sources without attributing the copied chunks as quotation. After discovering this in a large number of works, he reported his findings to several people in authority.

A large-scale scandal which attracted a great deal of public attention ensued. The outcomes included:

- Plagiarism was discovered in dozens of engineering PhD theses and master's dissertations. It consisted primarily of material from and in introductions, and often the writers were international students.
- Many of the students affected were told to decide whether to have their degrees withdrawn, or to admit to the plagiarism and be given an opportunity to re-write (an option of challenging the accusation of plagiarism before an internal university body was also offered).
- The positions of the supervisors involved were negatively affected in a number of ways, including losing the right to supervise research students. One lost an endowed chair.

- The professor who lost his chair sued the university, which had to pay him significant compensation.

Various actors in and commentators on the scandal put forward the following perspectives (their accounts come from a detailed report in the *Chronicle of Higher Education*, Wasley, 2006).

Two academics who were commissioned to investigate and write a report concluded that the supervisors 'either failed to monitor the writing in their advisees' theses or simply ignored academic honesty, integrity, and basically supported academic fraudulence'.

One of the students who was threatened with revocation of his degree said that the questionable parts of his work were

> not plagiarism . . . [arguing] that those making the charges are not familiar with engineering theses . . . [and that they] have missed the page in the fourth chapter . . . with a crucial reference that explains why the next twelve pages of text and calculations are nearly identical to ones in a thesis written by another student.

One of the supervisors involved commented that the problem was carelessness leading to forgotten references or quotation marks, that 'there was no intention to deceive, and therefore no plagiarism'.

The same supervisor expressed a view that 'at any university, at any department, I think you would find the same'.

Another staff member in the department said that 'most of the plagiarism . . . occurred in introductory chapters describing research methods and reviewing the previous literature, for which there is little expectation of originality'.

Discussion

- Four actors mentioned above give five perspectives on the situation, some of which are mutually contradictory. According to the facts in the case presented here, which perspectives seem closest to reality?
- Was the response to the affected students a reasonable one? Were there alternative approaches?
- How could the situation have been prevented?

Read more about the case

Ohio University Compass (2010) Jay S. Gunasekera public name-clearing hearing [WWW Document]. URL http://www.ohio.edu/compass/stories/10-11/9/Jay-Gunasekera-name-clearing-814.cfm

Pyle, E. (2011) OU, professor settle plagiarism lawsuit. *The Columbus Dispatch.* http://www.dispatch.com/content/stories/local/2011/03/08/OU-plagiarism-settlement.html

Wasley, P. (2006) The Plagiarism Hunter, *Chronicle of Higher Education*, 8/11/2006, Vol. 52, Issue 49. http://chronicle.com/article/The-Plagiarism- Hunter/5109/

Case 3: Who owns student work?

Turnitin is a provider of a text-matching service which was in use at a secondary school in the US state of Virginia and at another school in Arizona in 2007 when students at those schools brought a lawsuit against Turnitin's parent company, iParadigms.

The students had been obliged to submit their work to Turnitin as a condition of it being assessed; had they not done so, they would not have received a grade on their work. In submitting the work, the students clicked to agree acceptance of Turnitin's terms and conditions. However, they included a statement at the beginning of their assignments that they did not want their assignments to become part of Turnitin's database, and thereby be used for comparison against work which other students would later submit to Turnitin. Despite those statements, the students' written assignments were stored in Turnitin's archive, and the students claimed copyright infringement.

Turnitin entered counterclaims against the students. One of these was an attempt to recover from the students the costs they incurred in defending themselves against the lawsuit. The basis for this was their usage policy (part of a separate document, not part of the terms and conditions) which provided for such indemnification.

The judgement issued in the case denied both the counterclaims and the students' original claim against iParadigms. A factor in the decision was that the students' proviso that their work could not form part of Turnitin's database was an attempt to modify the agreement they had accepted by clicking, but that agreement specified that the terms could not be modified. The judgement also found that Turnitin's use of the students' work did not constitute copyright infringement in that it was transformative:

> Plaintiffs originally created and produced their works for the purpose of education and creative expression. iParadigms, through Turnitin, uses the papers for an entirely different purpose, namely, to prevent plagiarism and protect the students' written works from plagiarism.
>
> (Hilton, 2008: 13)

Discussion

In this case, students brought a complaint against the provider of a text-matching tool to which their school had decided student work should be submitted. In the context of a discussion between the school and these students, what arguments do you imagine the students would present to explain their position? What arguments do you think the school might counter with, to explain their insistance on the use of Turnitin?

Read more about the case

Hilton, C.M. (2008) AV *et al.* v. iParadigms. US District Court for the Eastern District of Virginia.

Glod, M. (2007, March 29). McLean students sue anti-cheating service. *The Washington Post*. Retrieved from http://www.washingtonpost.com/wp dyn/content/article/2007/03/28/AR2007032802038.html

Case 4: Deciding what to report

Unlike the first three cases presented in this section, this case is fictionalised.

Peter was a lecturer in business management and had assigned his students to carry out a project in groups and present the results in a written report. The report was to be written up as a draft and read by another group of students who would offer peer feedback. Each group would then make an oral presentation of their findings to the whole class, followed by a period of questions aimed at helping them tighten up their report. They would then revise their written report and turn it in to the teacher for a grade. The grade would be based only on the report in its final written form, but a precondition for the work to be assessed was that the group had gone through each step in the process.

A few days before the oral presentations, a group of students came to see Peter in his office. They were concerned and upset because the report which they were providing feedback on contained what they believed was plagiarism. The literature review contained paragraphs which they had discovered had been copied from several sources.

Peter viewed the copied language as unacceptable but did not diagnose it as deceptive plagiarism. He told the students that they had done well to spot the problem and that they should bring it up in the question period following the oral presentation. He believed that members of other groups could benefit from hearing the matter raised as well.

After leaving Peter's office, the students discussed the matter amongst themselves and became more upset still. They believed that their classmates had engaged in deceptive plagiarism and, had they succeeded, would have distorted the grading curve, resulting in a relatively lower award for their own work. They also believed that it was Peter's responsibility to report cheating, and that he was trying to evade an unpleasant duty.

Instead of bringing the matter up after the oral presentations, the students made a formal report against their peers to the office in the university responsible for academic integrity. That office began an investigation against the potential offenders. At the same time, they began an investigation against Peter.

The terms of Peter's contract, like all other teachers at his university, stipulated that he was required to report any attempt to cheat. A high-level administrator decided that by not reporting the possible plagiarism, Peter had breached his contract, and began proceedings to dismiss him. There followed a period of months when Peter was called to hearings to explain his actions and motivations in the matter. Eventually Peter was issued a warning and allowed to keep his job. Although he felt unfairly treated, he accepted that outcome as the best way of ending the matter and moving on.

Discussion

The disagreement in this case was not over whether deceptive plagiarism should be reported. From Peter's perspective it was about whether his decision that deception was not involved could be second guessed. From the perspective of the university administration, whose position implied a firm conviction that deceptive plagiarism had been involved, it was about whether a teacher had infinite latitude either to reach an unsound decision or to avoid taking unpleasant action by hiding behind a pretence that deception had not been involved. To the extent that deception is a factor in plagiarism, what latitude do, or should, teachers have to make such a determination? What scope do, or should, universities have to constrain their choices?

Case 5: 'A hired gun'

In 2010 an article appeared in the *Chronicle of Higher Education* authored (under a pseudonym) by a ghost author, a man who writes student assignments on commission. In this article, which attracted a great deal of press attention, 'Ed Dante' made the following points about the service he provides and the people who use it:

- He and his colleagues are very prolific and very much in demand: 'On any day of the academic year, I am working on upward of 20 assignments'.
- His services are in demand from three groups, the very wealthy, students who are not adequately prepared for university education, and speakers of English as a second language. About the latter two groups he says: 'colleges are failing them utterly'.

- A common task is doing students' work on distant courses, from taking part in on-line seminars to taking exams.
- The students who use his services are so numerous that all university teachers have encountered one: My customers are your students. I promise you that. Somebody in your classroom uses a service that you can't detect, that you can't defend against, that you may not even know exists.
- That the situation is at least partly the fault of staff: 'For those of you who have ever mentored a student through the writing of a dissertation, served on a thesis-review committee, or guided a graduate student through a formal research process, I have a question: Do you ever wonder how a student who struggles to formulate complete sentences in conversation manages to produce marginally competent research? How does that student get by you?'

Discussion

- Why are Dante's services so popular?
- What measures can teachers take to keep students from hiring someone like Ed Dante?
- What measures can universities take?
- If universities are failing students from non-traditional backgrounds and L2 speakers, what is the solution?
- How reflective of your reality is his belief that every classroom has a student who uses someone like him?
- The implication of the question 'How does that student get by you?' seems to be that if staff were more alert and challenged students who produce surprising results, there might be fewer students who get away with using his service. To what extent is that implied criticism a fair one?

Read more about the case

Dante, E. (2010) The Shadow Scholar. *Chronicle of Higher Education.* URL http://chronicle.com/article/The-Shadow-Scholar/125329/

Case 6: What kind of plagiarism? Part I

This case study and the next present the work of writers who used their sources in ways which many teachers would consider textual plagiarism. They form part of the data for a larger study (Pecorari, 2003; Pecorari, 2006). They are presented here for you to decide whether they constitute prototypical plagiarism. These cases are divided into four parts: background about the writer; information about and examples of how sources were used; the writer's responses in our interview about source use; and the supervisor's view. Pause after reading each of these parts and assess what you think about these students, and about how you evaluate their source use.

Part A: The writer

Helen was a master's student from Taiwan studying in the UK when we met. She was writing a dissertation on language learning, and volunteered to take part in my research which involved interviews with both her and her supervisor, and an analysis of part of her dissertation in draft form. Helen was interested in how children learn language, and spoke with apparent enthusiasm in our interviews about going back to Taiwan and teaching there. For the time being, though, she was wholeheartedly engaged in writing her dissertation.

Part B: The dissertation

The text Helen gave me for analysis was 3,510 words long, and was the draft that was intended to form part of her master's dissertation. There were 28 citations to 16 sources in it. I was able to compare just over 1,000 words of her text to her sources. There were several reasons in this study overall why some parts of the students' texts could not be compared to sources. One was, naturally, that some portions were averrals, rather than attributions, and there was no source, ostensibly, with which they could be compared. Another was that the source was not available. A third was that the referencing information was so unclear that it was not possible to know what the source was. Where possible I asked the student for clarification, but they were frequently unsure as well.

Looking at the parts of Helen's text which I could compare to her sources, exactly half of the words in it were taken from her sources. Eleven per cent were quotation, and the other 39% were not identified as quotation. Although signalled quotations were relatively infrequent in Helen's work, references to her sources were present much more regularly. In addition, she worked with the language of her sources, stitching segments from different sources together and making changes to them in a patchwriting strategy. These examples give a representative cross-section of the passages from her text which were compared with their sources. In each of these cases, the source Helen cites is actually the one she used.

Helen
In teaching non-native speakers, teachers might introduce new vocabulary which learners already know its cultural and linguistic background knowledge (Taylor, 1990: 6).

Source (Taylor, 1990)
In teaching non-native speakers, then, we might introduce new vocabulary into the context of what our learners already know, culturally as well as linguistically.

> **Helen**
> In addition to gap-filling, there should be a variety of techniques to practise new words, such as word class change, crossword completion, crossword creation, multiple choice, sentence creation from a table, etc. (Williams and Dallas, 1984: 205).
>
> **Source: (Williams and Dallas, 1984)**
> Each unit of the workbook also contains a 'Using New Words' Section, employing a variety of techniques in addition to gap-filling, such as word class change, crossword completion, crossword creation, multiple choice, sentence creation from a table, etc.
>
> **Helen**
> Carter and McCarthy (1988) point out eight questions that teachers and students often ask about vocabulary and language study. One of them is whether some words are more useful than others to beginning learners in second or foreign language learning (Carter and McCarthy, 1988:1).
>
> **Source (Carter and McCarthy, 1988)**
> It may be useful, however, to begin this chapter by listing some questions which teachers and students have asked, usually quite persistently, about vocabulary and language study.//3. In the early stages of learning a second or foreign language, are some words more useful to the learner than others?

Part C: Helen's account

Helen's perception was that all three of these excerpts from her work were examples of paraphrase. She said that she chose to paraphrase the first of these, Taylor, because she did not want to have too many quotations in her work. She described her process of paraphrasing the Taylor passage: 'I think I delete some unnecessary words'.

Doing a paraphrase like this was hard, she said; she estimated that it would take five to ten minutes to convert the passage in Taylor into the form in which it appeared in her text. Although the changes to the source are not radical – her wording still retains the phrases 'In teaching non-native speakers', 'might introduce new vocabulary' and 'learners already know' – in the space of this short passage she has introduced a syntactic irregularity ('which learners already know its') and an unfortunate wording ('learners know its knowledge').

Part D: The Supervisor's account

The reaction of Helen's supervisor could perhaps be called mild, unsurprised unhappiness. For example, looking at the middle of the three extracts above, he felt she had misrepresented the source to some extent, since they were describing a specific book and she was using the reference to them to support a claim about what books generally should contain. He also thought she should have used quotation marks because 'I mean it is lifted. So if she'd put in "there should be a variety", if she'd put quotation around there beginning at "a variety" then you'd have less problem with it'.

On balance he did not see the source use in Helen's text as constituting a significant problem:

> Overall, the data itself is much more important than getting this stuff wrong. Assuming that she's not lifting . . . she may be, I don't know, but the thing is, she's not lifting great chunks of the stuff, and not understanding it, I mean, that's the problem. In a sense, if she's doing it and understanding it more or less, which is why it will be interesting to see when she expands this, then that would be a problem, but if she's doing it and she is actually understanding it, that's fine.

Like the Turkish scientists and others quoted earlier in this book, Helen's supervisor drew a distinction between her results and her patchwriting, and thought the former were 'much more important'. However, he did characterise the language she had repeated from the source as 'lifting', which is a common euphemism for stealing. He also sent mixed signals about whether it was plagiarism, bringing up the word only to dismiss it:

> So *this* sort of lifting, plagiarism, I wouldn't say, again, especially since she has got the quote and the page number, I wouldn't get terribly upset about. I mean, [it] wouldn't fail the dissertation. But it would bring it down a bit.

Discussion

Helen's discussion of her own source use showed that she was making conscious choices, that she was choosing to paraphrase, or to come as close to it as possible, because she felt too much quotation would not be appropriate. If we accept her account, the changes she made to her sources cost her a great deal of time and effort. Helen's supervisor was not happy about the way she used sources, but neither was he terribly unhappy.

- Is Helen's source use acceptable or unacceptable? If the latter, is it plagiarism?
- How would you react to it if you were her supervisor? What would you tell her?
- If Helen is accurate in her account of the time she spent paraphrasing each chunk like the ones above, and considering the problematic language she introduced into her text where she tried to make changes, does she have any realistic alternatives to this strategy?

Case 6: What kind of plagiarism? Part II

Part A: The writer

Erden was a master's student in biology at the time he took part in my study. He had come to the UK from Turkey, where he had worked as a research scientist, and had had some experience writing up his research findings both in English and in Turkish.

Erden was writing a demanding dissertation to a tight schedule, juggling the writing with coursework and laboratory work, and spending what time he could with his family, who had travelled to the UK with him. The impression he gave though was that while the demands on his time and abilities were challenging, he was rising to them: his did not appear to be a 'not waving but drowning' scenario.

That spirit of quiet accomplishment of the necessary was what he portrayed when we discussed his writing. Writing was laborious, especially so in English, but he could do it. His confidence seemed to be based to a large extent on the fact that he felt in control of his research.

Erden provided me with a draft of a literature review which was to be incorporated later into his dissertation. After our first interview, when I had expressed an interest in his sources, he realised that I would have difficulty finding many of them as they were pre-prints which had reached him through his supervisor. On that realisation, he offered me the loan of his sources, which were journal articles and conference paper, so that I could make copies.

Part B: The dissertation

Erden's text was 1373 words long, and contained 20 citations to 18 sources. I was able to compare 80% of it to his sources. In keeping with the highly visible convention in the natural sciences, Erden's text contained no direct, signalled quotation. However, within the passages I compared, 73% of the words came from Erden's sources. Parts were more extensively paraphrased than others. The examples below give the flavour of Erden's processes, and hint at the variation in just how source-dependent the components of his text were.

Erden
Van den Houwe, I. (1998) has suggested that cryopreservation is very important on the conservation of *Musa* germplasm.

Source (Van den Houwe *et al.* 1998 – a header)
The in vitro germplasm collection at the Musa INIBAP Transit Centre and the importance of cryopreservation

---

Erden

Van and Kitto (1990) reported that plant regeneration from callus cultures of *Mentha* depended on explant source, genotype and culture medium component. They cultured mature embryo, seedlings, and flower parts on a MS medium. Cultured shoots regenerated on mature peppermint embryo on medium that contained BA 0.5 mg/l and 0.5 mg/l NAA.

Source (Van Eck and Kitto, 1990)

Plant regeneration from callus cultures of mint depended on explant source, genotype, and culture medium components. Mature embryos, seedling and flower parts, as well as chilled or desiccated immature embryos of peppermint (*Mentha piperita* L.) and spearmint (*Mentha spicata* L.) were cultured on a Murashige-Skoog medium containing various combinations of growth factors. Shoots regenerated from callus that developed either on mature peppermint embryos cultured on medium that contained BA at 0.5 mg/liter $^{-1}$ and NAA at 0.5 mg/liter $^{-1}$ or on immature peppermint embryos

Erden

Faure *et al.* (1998) determined that in-vitro shoot Organo-genesis of peppermint and spearmint was obtained from leaf discs. Best result were obtained when explants were cultured for two weeks onto MS medium supplementing with 300mm mannitol, 2.0 mm BA and 2.0 mm IBA and then transferred on a medium without mannitol and containing 0.5 mm NAA. 9.0 mm BA and 0.5 mm TDZ. They achieved 78% regeneration for peppermint and 49% spearmint.

Source (Faure *et al.*, 1998)

In vitro shoot organogenis of peppermint and spearmint was obtained from leaf disks.//Best results were obtained when explants were cultured for two weeks onto Murashige and Skoog medium supplemented with 300 mM mannitol, 2.0 μM 6-benzyladenine and 2.0 μM indole-3-butyric acid, and then transferred on a medium without mannitol and containing 0.5 μM α-naphthaleneacetic acid, 9.0 μM 6-benzyladenine and 0.5 μM thidiazuron. Using these culture conditions, percentages of regeneration were 78% for peppermint and 49% for spearmint.

Erden

Plant tissue culture storage methodology has been under development for some 15–20 years. During that time, considerable progress has been made, particularly in the cryopreservation of living organism.

Source (Withers, 1991b)

Plant tissue culture storage methodology has been under development for some 15–20 years. During that time, considerable progress has been made, particularly in the cryopreservation of living organisms in general and of plant material in particular. (Ashwood-Smith and Farrant, 1980; Kartha, 1985; Grout and Morris, 1987).

Erden's use of sources presents several features of note. First, his most common strategy is to condense the material he takes from a source, as he has done in the second example. Although Erden never signals the use of language from a source with quotation marks, he does give a citation to his source in most cases, throughout his writing sample. One of the few exceptions is the last example, above. Although there are too few passages in Erden's text without a citation to be able to find patterns with any degree of confidence, the last example here may not be atypical in that it – the only one of the four that does not name a source – is also the only one of the four which reports somebody else's work. Withers, the source of the last example, makes a statement about a trend in recent research in the field and cites three sources for it. Erden repeats the claim, but not the citations. However, in the other three examples, it is the sources' own research being reported, and Erden cites them.

Although he names his sources in the majority of cases, there are often surface inaccuracies. In the first example above he used a paper by van den Houwe *et al.*, but gave the authorship as just van den Houwe. The second example makes use of a source authored by van Eck and Kitto, but Erden identifies the first author only as 'Van'. These and other relatively minor issues give the impression that he saw this draft very much as a work in progress.

Part C: Erden's account

When we met for an interview to talk about his text, Erden showed me a pack of index cards on which he took notes. Each of the articles he had read was summarised onto a card, and he said that when he wrote his literature review, he generally worked from the index cards, going back to the article only if there was a detail he did not remember.

In our first interview Erden had himself introduced the topic of plagiarism and said how careful he felt he needed to be to cite sources appropriately. Having seen his text in between, I asked him during our second interview how confident he felt that the had managed to follow the conventions for citation. His answer confirmed that the draft we were discussing was a candidate for future revision:

I've cited all the literature which I used, but probably **at the first stage**, maybe, I haven't paid attention if it's direct citation, maybe altered sentence or not. (emphasis added)

There is then presumably going to be a later stage when Erden will work with his sources and pay attention to whether he has used direct quotation or has altered sentences. However, it may not be an easy process to carry out because Erden is 'not sure' about the sources of the text we look at:

> because I can't remember, you know, when you are taking a note, sometimes you just copied a sentence, or sometimes you summarized a paragraph, and after sometimes later you could not remember, you just copied this sentence or you just make a summary.

We then turned to the subject of why he had chosen to cite the sources he did, and his answers came so easily that it was manifestly a topic he had thought about before. One of the references to a method of preserving germ plasm was the one he was going to use in his experiments, and so he had mentioned it in his literature review to prepare the way for discussing it in his methods section. The picture that emerged as we spoke was that he had read relevant sources, understood them, and cited them because they served a purpose, but he had not arrived at a point in the process of constructing his text where he anticipated that would be obvious to the reader. He had done the equivalent of a camper who lays a tent, and the tent poles and the stakes and the hammer on the ground in approximately the right place. Actually erecting the tent will be a last step in the process, and with the preparations made, a minor if an important one. With chunks from his sources distributed where they would do most good, all Erden had to do was pull them into order and work out whether the text he had copied from his note cards into his draft was 'just one sentence [taken directly from the source] or is it summary of the paragraph?'

As we talked, and looked at his text and at his sources, Erden noticed a chunk which had been copied, and was slightly surprised – but only slightly:

> I just see that now. But it is normal, while we are taking a note . . . you can copy it in your papers, sometimes you can copy directly to the sentence and sometimes summary.

And while he would like in an ideal world to tidy up these loose ends, it is not realistic to think he will. He cannot go back and check every citation

> because probably I am going to use hundreds of citations, hundreds of articles, I cannot go by sentence and sentence, which is . . . I mean, my position, it is impossible.

Part D: The supervisor's account

If Erden had both an awareness and a resigned acceptance of the fact that his source use was less than ideal, he may have inherited it from his supervisor. The two were certainly singing off the same page. Very close to the beginning of our interview, and before we had a chance to look at Erden's sources, the supervisor commented on the intertextual influences which he assumed were at work on the draft:

> In this case I don't think there's a problem but you can clearly identify two different forms of the writing here. One is where he's very much quoting in the introduction, the first two paragraphs particularly, from other people who might have written similar introductions but obviously when he gets into the literature review on *Mentha*, given that there isn't very much that's being done specifically on *Mentha*, that's much more his own writing and you can tell by reading it that it is.

The supervisor understood, in other words, that Erden was repeating from his sources. In characterising that repetition, he moved nearer to and further from the idea of 'quoting' several times. Erden was 'very much quoting in the introduction' but when I asked how he knew it was a quotation (given that my background has led me to regard a quotation as something signalled as such) he pulled back from the word: 'well, not a quotation, maybe a precis or something like that and a slight modification'. However, in the next sentence he readopted it, saying 'what he's doing here is quoting Roberts, so I would have expected that to be fairly similar to what Roberts has written somewhere'.

This is significant for how it clashes with the received view of quotation, standardised in instruction sheets and warnings about plagiarism, saying that quotation is something which is signalled as such, and further which is a verbatim repetition from the source. But what Erden has done, in his supervisor's mind, neither is nor is not quotation, but it is definitely a modification of the source. A second significant point in this is that the supervisor realises that Erden's work is not literally quotation, at least not in the usual understanding of the word; his repeated adoption and denial of the word indicates that. However, by adopting it metaphorically, he claims for Erden's work something of the legitimacy associated with quotation, as opposed to patchwriting. He is also aware, though, that many people would not consider this strategy fully legitimate:

> I would be concerned if there were quite a few paragraphs like that throughout the thesis which I could specifically identify as being word to word from somewhere else, then I would be objecting.

Once again, the distinction between the introduction and the findings arises. Ideally the dissertation should not 'sort of paraphrase exactly what other people have written' but Erden's approach to the task has not been 'out of line'. And when he gets on to writing up his findings, 'it's virtually guaranteed to have the student's own work, certainly in this particular case, because nobody's done what he's done before, so he's going to be writing original stuff'. Provided he has 'original stuff' in his findings, a certain amount of patchwriting in the introduction is to be tolerated, if not encouraged.

Discussion

Individual understandings of academic conventions for source use vary widely, but in this case Erden and his supervisor were in broad agreement that Erden's quasi-quotation from his sources was not ideal but not catastrophic. How do you evaluate the way Erden has used his sources in the examples above? Is it acceptable or not? If not, is it plagiarism or something else?

If you think that Erden's use of sources is not acceptable, how would you explain to him why not? What would you advise him to do in place of his current strategy?

Erden's supervisor made the point that his patchwriting in the beginning of his dissertation had to be considered in the light of his findings, which were predicted to be original. To what extent do you agree with that reasoning?

Earlier cases examined accusations of plagiarism against an undergraduate in the UK and a large number of postgraduates in the US. If Erden were at either of those institutions, would he get the same response to his work as he got from his supervisor?

Appendix C   Sources of examples

The sources of the examples used in Chapters 1–10 are identified here, apart from those which come from students who participated in my research and shared their texts with me on the understanding that they would be anonymous.

Example 1.1 (and 10.1)
http://www.calendar.soton.ac.uk/sectionIV/academic-integrity-statement.html;

Example 1.2
http://www.studentgroups.ucla.edu/dos/assets/documents/StudentGuide.pdf
The same definition also appears here: http://guides.library.ucla.edu/citing;

Example 1.3
http://www.victoria.ac.nz/home/study/plagiarism#what-is-plagiarism

Example 1.4
Milan, E. P., Malheiros, E. S., Fischman, O., and Lopes Colombo, A. (1997) Evaluation of the Auxacolor system for the identification of clinical yeast isolates. *Mycopathologia*, 137, 153–157.

Example 1.5
Nokkala, E. (2010) Passion as the foundation of natural law in the German enlightenment: Johann Jacob Schmauss and J.H.G. von Justi. *European Review of History*, 17, 113–123.

Example 1.6
Smith, G. C. S. (2003) Parachute use to prevent death and major trauma related to gravitational challenge: systematic review of randomised controlled trials. *BMJ*, 327(7429), 1459–1461. doi:10.1136/bmj.327.7429.1459

Example 1.7
The student text is anonymous. The student's source was:

Chambers, H. L. and Hummer, K. E. (1994) Chromosome counts in the *Mentha* collection at the USDA-ARS National Clonal Germplasm Repository. *Taxon*, 43: 423–432.

Example 1.8

The student text is anonymous. The student's source was:

Reed, B. M. (1999) In vitro storage conditions for mint germ plasm. *HortScience*, 34: 350–352.

Example 1.9

The student text is anonymous. The student's source was:

Kennard, W. C., Slocum, M, K., Figdore, S. S., Osborn, T. C. (1994) Genetic analysis of morphological variation in *Brassica oleracea* using molecular markers. *Theoretical Applied Genetics*, 87, 721–732.

Example 4.1a

The student text is anonymous.

Example 4.1b

Pyle, D. W. and Sayers, T. A. (1980) A BEd course for serving teachers: An evaluation of the first year. *British Journal of Inservice Education*, 7, 10–37.

Example 4.2

The student text is anonymous. The student's source was:

Grimmett, P. P. and Crehan, E. P. (1992) The nature of collegiality in teacher development, in: M. Fullan and A. Hargreaves (eds), *Teacher development and educational change*. London: Falmer Press, pp. 56–85.

Example 4.3

Smith, M. and Taffler, R. J. (2000) The chairman's statement: A content analysis of discretionary narrative disclosures. *Accounting, Auditing and Accountability Journal*, 13(5), 624–647. doi:10.1108/09513570010353738

Example 4.4

Newton, M. (1993) Styles and strategies of evaluating INSET, in: R. G. Burgess, J. Connor, S. Galloway, M. Morrison and M. Newton (eds) *Implementing in-service education and training*. London: Routledge, pp. 8–38.

Chapter 5, Task 1

Myers, D.G. (2007) *Psychology*. (8th edition) Worth, New York, NY.

Chapter 5, Task 2

The student text is anonymous. The student's source was:

Watkins, C. (1985) Does pastoral care = personal and social education? *Pastoral Care*, 3 (3), 179–183.

Example 8.1
Du, W., Coaker, M., Sobel, J. D., and Akins, R. A. (2004) Shuttle vectors for Candida albicans, Ta: control of plasmid copy number and elevated expression of cloned genes. *Current Genetics*, 45(6), 390–398. doi:10.1007/s00294-004-0499-3, pp. 390–391

Example 8.2
Holmes, J. (2006) Sharing a laugh: Pragmatic aspects of humor and gender in the workplace. *Journal of Pragmatics*, 38(1), 26–50. doi:10.1016/j.pragma.2005.06.007 p. 30

Example 8.3
This is a modified version of Example 8.1.

Example 8.4
Mowlds, P. and Kavanagh, K. (2007) Effect of pre-incubation temperature on susceptibility of Galleria mellonella larvae to infection by Candida albicans. *Mycopathologia*, 165, 5–12.

Example 8.5
De la Rosa, J., Ruiz, T., and Rodriguez, L. (2000) Cloning and Characterization of a Candida albicans Gene Homologous to Fructose-1,6-Bisphosphatase Genes. *Current Microbiology*, 41(6), 384–387. doi:10.1007/s002840010154

Example 8. 6
Henriques, M., Gasparettl, K., Azeredo, J., and Oliveira, R. (2002) Experimental methodology to quantify Candida albicans cell surface hydrophobicity. *Biotechnology Letters*, 24, 1111–1115.

Examples 8.6a and 8.6b
These are modified versions of Example 8.6.

Example 10.2
http://academicregistry.glam.ac.uk/documents/download/215/

Example 10.3
http://wise.xmu.edu.cn/english/viewNews.asp?id=570

Example 10.4
http://helioscollege.com/menu/studying-at-hic/129/129/1?phpMyAdmin=c5b2348c822a59542c66f24c75b2f043&phpMyAdmin=7190c382d478d57352bda6a2a7322f8f

Example 10.5
http://library.csusm.edu/plagiarism/howtoavoid/how_avoid_common.htm

Example 10.6
http://www.admin.cam.ac.uk/univ/plagiarism/students/referencing/
commonknowledge.html

Example 10.7
http://www.usg.edu/galileo/skills/unit08/credit08_04.phtml

Example 10.8
http://www.lib.usm.edu/legacy/plag/whatisplag.php

Example 10.9
Associated British Foods (2007) *Annual report.*

Example 10.10
Marks and Spencer (2002) *Annual report.*

Example 10.11
British American Tobacco (2011) *Annual report.*

Examples 10.12 and 10.13
Aggrekko (2007–2009) *Annual report.*

Example 10.14
Aggrekko (2000–2001) *Annual report.*

Notes

i   Examples of policy, guidance about plagiarism, and good, questionable and bad citation practice are given throughout this book. The policies and other regulatory documents quoted from are identified in Appendix C. Although these are quoted in part for the purpose of showing where current practices are inadequate, no direct criticism of them is intended; criticism, where it is implied, is aimed at the current received practice across universities. The sources of examples of good citation practice are also identified in Appendix C. Examples of questionable or poor citation practice come from my research corpus and are used with the permission of the writers, on the condition that they remain anonymous. Some examples feature both an extract from a piece of student writing and the student's source, but that source is not always acknowledged in the student writing. The conclusion that these were in fact the sources the students drew on was drawn on the basis of textual evidence and details provided by the students themselves. Further details are given in Pecorari, 2003.

ii A pseudonym, as are the names of all of my research participants mentioned in this book.

iii http://www.writing.utoronto.ca/images/stories/Documents/how-not-to-plagiarize.pdf

iv English is dominant as a global lingua franca in academic life, as well as in many other domains, and the numbers of individuals working or studying in English as a second or foreign language are large. However, in principle nearly everything which is said in this chapter about that group is equally true of anyone studying in a language which is not their first, whatever that language may be.

v   The sources of these examples are identified in Appendix 2, but the names of the universities are not used here because it is my purpose to use them as examples of common practice, not to single them out.

Bibliography

Abasi, A. R. and Graves, B. (2008) Academic literacy and plagiarism: Conversations with international graduate students and disciplinary professors. *Journal of English for Academic Purposes*, 7, 221–233.

American Psychological Association (2010) *Publication manual of the American Psychological Association*. American Psychological Association, Washington, DC.

Angélil-Carter, S. (2000) *Stolen language? Plagiarism in writing*. Longman, Harlow.

Ashworth, P., Bannister, P. and Thorne, P. (1997) Guilty in whose eyes? University students' perceptions of cheating and plagiarism in academic work and assessment. *Studies in Higher Education* 22, 187–203.

Ashworth, P., Freewood, M. and Macdonald, R. (2003) The student lifeworld and the meanings of plagiarism. *Journal of Phenomenological Psychology*, 34, 258–278.

Austen, J. (1813/1995) *Pride and prejudice*. New York: Modern Library. Retrieved from http://site.ebrary.com/id/5002014

Badge, J. L., Cann, A. J. and Scott, J. (2007) To cheat or not to cheat? A trial of the JISC Plagiarism Detection Service with biological sciences students. *Assessment and Evaluation in Higher Education*, 32, 433–439.

Bakhtin, M. M. (1986) *Speech genres and other late essays* (Vol. 8). Austin: University of Texas Press.

Ballard, B. and Clanchy, J. (1991) Assessment by misconception: Cultural influences and intellectual traditions, in: L. Hamp-Lyons (ed.), *Assessing writing in academic contexts*. Ablex, Norwood, NJ, pp. 19–35.

Barker, J. (1997) The purpose of study, attitudes to study and staff-student relationships, in: D. McNamara and R. Harris (eds), *Overseas Students in Higher Education: Issues in teaching and learning*. Routledge, London, pp. 108–123.

Barks, D. and Watts, P. (2001) Textual borrowing strategies for graduate-level ESL writers, in: D. Belcher and A. Hirvela (eds), *Linking literacies: Perspectives on L2 reading-writing connections*. Ann Arbor: University of Michigan Press, 246–267.

Baty, P. (2004) 'Plagiarist student to sue university'. *The Times Online*. Retrieved January 19, 2006, from http://www.timesonline.co.uk/article/0,,3561-1126250,00.html.

BBC News (2003) High costs "causing student plagiarism". URL http://news.bbc.co.uk/2/hi/uk_news/education/3072061.stm

Becher, T. (1989) *Academic tribes and territories: Intellectual enquiry and the cultures of disciplines*. Milton Keynes: Society for Research into Higher Education and Open University Press.

Becher, T. and Trowler, P. R. (2001) (2nd edition) *Academic tribes and territories: Intellectual enquiry and the culture of disciplines*. Milton Keynes: Open University Press.

Belcher, D. (2001) Cyberdiscourse, evolving notions of authorship, and the teaching of writing, in: M. Hewings (ed.), *Academic writing in context: Implications and applications*. Birmingham: University of Birmingham Press, pp. 140–149.

Bennett, R. (2005) Factors associated with student plagiarism in a post-1992 university. *Assessment and Evaluation in Higher Education*, 30, 137–162.

Benson, P. and Heidish, P. (1995) The ESL technical expert: Writing processes and classroom practices, in: D. Belcher and G. Braine (eds), *Academic writing in a second language: Essays on research and pedagogy*. Norwood, NJ: Ablex, pp. 313–330.

Betts, D. D. (1992) Retraction of an article published in *The Canadian Journal of Physics*. *The Canadian Journal of Physics*, 70, 289.

Biggs, J. B. (1996) Enhancing teaching through constructive alignment. *Higher Education*, 32, 347–364.

Bloch, J. (2001) Plagiarism and the ESL student: From printed to electronic texts, in: D. Belcher and A. Hirvela (eds), *Linking Literacies: Perspectives on L2 reading-writing connections*. University of Michigan Press, Ann Arbor, MI, pp. 209–228.

Bloch, J. (2008) Plagiarism in an intercultural rhetoric context: What we can learn about one from the other, in: U. Connor, E. Nagelhout and W. Rozycki (eds), *Contrastive Rhetoric: Reaching to intercultural rhetoric*. John Benjamins, Amsterdam, pp. 257–274.

Bloch, J. (2012) *Plagiarism, intellectual property and the teaching of L2 composition*. Multilingual Matters, Bristol.

Blum, S. (2010) *My word! Plagiarism and college culture*. Cornell University Press, Ithaca, NY.

Bourdieu, P. and Passeron, J.-C. (1965) Introduction: Langage et rapport au langage dans la situation pédagogique, in: P. Bourdieu, J.-C. Passeron and M. de Saint Martin (eds), *Rapport pédagogique et communication*. Paris: Mouton.

Bradbury, M. (1959/1976) *Eating people is wrong*. Secker and Warburg, London.

Breen, L. and Maassen, M. (2005) Reducing the incidence of plagiarism in an undergraduate course. *Issues in Educational Research*, 15, 1–16.

Bretag, T. (2004) Implementing plagiarism policy in the internationalised university, in: *Educational integrity values in teaching, learning and research*. Presented at the 2nd Asia-Pacific Educational Integrity Conference, University of Newcastle, Newcastle, Australia.

British Council (2011) New international student trend presents fresh challenges for universities [WWW Document]. British Council. URL http://www.britishcouncil.org/press/new-international-student-trend-presents-fresh-challenges

Brown, A. S. and Murphy, D. R. (1989) Cryptomnesia: Delineating inadvertent plagiarism. *Journal of Experimental Psychology: Learning, Memory, and Cognition*, 15, 432–442.

Bryson, B. (2001) *Down under*. Black Swan, London.

Buranen, L. (1999) 'But I Wasn't Cheating': Plagiarism and Cross-cultural Mythology, in: L. Buranen and A. M. Roy (eds), *Perspectives on plagiarism and intellectual property in a postmodern world*. State University of New York Press, Albany, pp. 63–74.

Cammish, N. K. (1997) Through a glass darkly: Problems of studying at advanced level through the medium of English, in: D. McNamara and R. Harris (eds), *Overseas students in higher education: Issues in teaching and learning*. Routledge, London, pp. 143–155.

Carroll, J. and Appleton, J. (2005) Towards consistent penalty decisions for breaches of academic regulations in one UK university. *International Journal for Educational Integrity*, 1(1). Retrieved from http://www.ojs.unisa.edu.au/index.php/IJEI/article/view/15/5

Chicago Manual of Style, 16th edition (2010) University of Chicago Press, Chicago.

Culwin, F. and Lancaster, T. (2001) Plagiarism issues for higher education. *VINE*, 31(2), 36–41.

Currie, P. (1998) Staying out of trouble: Apparent plagiarism and academic survival. *Journal of Second Language Writing*, 7, 1–18.

Dante, E. (2010) The shadow scholar. *Chronicle of Higher Education.* URL http://chronicle.com/article/The-Shadow-Scholar/125329/

Davis, S. F., Grover, C. A., Becker, A. H. and McGregor, L. N. (1992) Academic dishonesty: Prevalence, determinants, techniques and punishments. *Teaching of Psychology,* 19, 17–20.

Davis, S. F. and Ludvigson, H. W. (1995) Additional data on academic dishonesty and a proposal for remediation. *Teaching of Psychology,* 22, 119–121.

Day, K. (2008) Time is not on our side: Plagiarism and workload in the community college, in: R. M. Howard and A. E. Robillard (eds), *Plagiarism: Identities, contexts, pedagogies.* Heinemann, Portsmouth, NH, pp. 43–61.

Deckert, G. D. (1993) Perspectives on plagiarism from ESL students in Hong Kong. *Journal of Second Language Writing,* 2(2), 131–148.

Department for Innovation, Universities and Skills (DIUS) (2008) Participation rates in higher education: Academic years 1999/2000–2006/2007 (Provisional) (No. DIUS SFR 02/2008).

Devitt, A. J. (1991) Intertextuality in tax accounting: Generic, referential, and functional, in: C. Bazerman and J. Paradis (eds), *Textual dynamics of the professions: Historical and contemporary studies of writing in professional communities.* University of Wisconsin Press, Madison, WI, pp. 336–357.

Devlin, M. (2006) Policy, preparation, and prevention: Proactive minimization of student plagiarism. *Journal of Higher Education Policy and Management,* 28, 45–58.

Dias, P. and Paré, A. (2000) *Transitions: Writing in academic and workplace settings.* Hampton Press, Cresskill, N.J.

Donahue, T. (2008) When copying Is not copying: Plagiarism and French composition scholarship, in: C. Eisner and M. Vicnius (eds), *Originality, Imitation, Plagiarism.* Ann Arbor: University of Michigan Press, pp. 90–103.

Elbow, P. (1999) Individualism and the teaching of writing: Response to Vai Ramanathan and Dwight Atkinson. *Journal of Second Language Writing,* 8, 327–338.

Eliot, T. S. (1920) *The sacred wood: Essays on poetry and criticism.* London: Methuen. Accessed at www.bartelby.com/200/ 2 July (2002).

Ellery, K. (2008a) An investigation into electronic-source plagiarism in a first-year essay assignment. *Assessment and Evaluation in Higher Education,* 33(6), 607–617.

Ellery, K. (2008b) Undergraduate plagiarism: a pedagogical perspective. *Assessment and Evaluation in Higher Education,* 33(5), 507–516.

Emerson, L. (2008) Plagiarism, a Turnitin trial and an experience of cultural disorientation, in: C. Eisner and M. Vicinus (eds), *Originality, imitation and plagiarism: Teaching writing in the digital age.* University of Michigan Press, Ann Arbor, MI, pp. 183–194.

England, A. (2008) The dynamic nature of common knowledge, in: C. Eisner and M. Vicinus (eds), *Originality, imitation and plagiarism: Teaching writing in the digital age.* University of Michigan Press, Ann Arbor, MI, pp. 104–113.

Errey, L. (2002) Plagiarism: Something fishy . . . or just a fish out of water? *Teaching Forum,* 50, 17–20.

Flowerdew, J. and Li, Y. (2007) Language re-use among Chinese apprentice scientists writing for publication. *Applied Linguistics,* 28, 440–465.

Franklyn-Stokes, A. and Newstead, S. E. (1995) Undergraduate cheating: who does what and why? *Studies in Higher Education,* 20, 39–52.

Gibaldi, J. (2009) *MLA handbook for writers of research papers, 7th edition.* Modern Language Association, New York.

Glod, M. (2007) McLean students sue anti-cheating service: Plaintiffs say company's database of term papers, essays violates copyright laws. *The Washington Post*, 29 March. Retrieved 29 September 2007 from http://www.washingtonpost.com/wp-dyn/content/article/2007/03/28/AR200703280(2038)html

Groom, N. (2000) Attribution and averral revisited: Three perspectives on manifest intertextuality in academic writing, in: P. Thompson (ed.), *Patterns and perspectives: Insights into EAP writing practice.* Centre for Applied Language Studies, Reading University, Reading, pp. 14–25.

Guardian (2004, 24 May) Plagiarising student sues university for negligence. *Guardian Unlimited.* http://education.guardian.co.uk/print/0,,4934062–108229,00.html

Ha, L. P. (2006) Plagiarism and overseas students: Stereotypes again? *ELT Journal*, 60, 76–78.

Hayes, N. and Introna, L. (2005) Cultural Values, Plagiarism and Fairness: When Plagiarism gets in the way of Learning. *Ethics and Behaviour*, 15(3), 213–231.

Hayes, N. and Introna, L. (2006) Systems for the production of plagiarists? The implications arising from the use of plagiarism detection systems in UK universities for Asian learners. *Journal of Academic Ethics*, 3, 55–73.

Hertz, N. (1985) *The end of the line: Essays on psychoanalysis and the sublime.* Columbia University Press, New York.

Hirvela, A. and Du, Q., forthcoming. 'Why am I paraphrasing?': Undergraduate ESL writers' engagement with source-based academic writing and reading. *Journal of English for Academic Purposes.*

Hofstede, G. (1984) *Culture's consequences: International differences in work-related values.* Sage, Newbury Park, CA.

Högskoleverket. (2011) *Disciplinära åtgärder mot studenter* [Disciplinary actions against students] (No. 2011:10 R). Stockholm.

Howard, R. M. (1995) Plagiarisms, authorships, and the academic death penalty. *College English*, 57, 788–805.

Howard, R. M. (1999) The new abolitionism comes to plagiarism, in: L. Buranen and A. M. Roy (eds), *Perspectives on plagiarism and intellectual property in a postmodern world.* State University of New York Press, Albany, pp. 87–95.

Howard, R. M. (2001) Conference on College Composition and Communication, Denver, CO (17 March).

Howard, R. M., Serviss, T. and Rodrigue, T. K. (2010) Writing from sources, writing from sentences. *Writing and Pedagogy*, 2(2), 177–192.

HSF (1993) *Högskoleförordning* [University ordinances] Chapter 10. Accessed 10 June 2009. Available at: http://www.notisum.se/rnp/SLS/LAG/19930100.html

Hull, G. and Rose, M. (1989) Rethinking remediation: Toward a social-cognitive understanding of problematic reading and writing. *Written Communication*, 6, 139–154.

Hunt, R. (n.d.) Four reasons to be happy about Internet plagiarism [WWW Document]. URL http://www.stu.ca/~hunt/4reasons.htm

Hyland, K. (2004) *Disciplinary discourses: Social interactions in academic writing.* Ann Arbor: University of Michigan Press.

IELTS (n.d.) IELTS band scores [WWW Document]. URL http://www.ielts.org/institutions/test_format_and_results/ielts_band_scores.aspx

Introna, L. and Hayes, N. (2007) Plagiarism detection systems and international students: detecting plagiarism, copying or learning?, in: T. Roberts (ed.), *Student plagiarism in an online world: Problems and solutions*, Idea Group, Hershey, PA.

Iyer, R. and Eastman, J. K. (2006) Academic dishonesty: Are business students different from other college students? *Journal of Education for Business*, 101–110.

Jamieson, S. (2008) One size does not fit all: Plagiarism across the curriculum, in: R. M. Howard and A. E. Robillard (eds), *Pluralizing plagiarism: Identities, contexts, pedagogies*. Boynton-Cook, Portsmouth, NH, pp. 77–91.

Jordan, R. R. (1997) *English for academic purposes: A guide and resource book for teachers*. Cambridge: Cambridge University Press.

Julliard, K. (1994) Perceptions of plagiarism in the use of other authors' language. *Family Medicine*, 26, 356–360.

Klitgård, I., Pecorari, D., Shaw, P. and McMillion, A. (2010, May) Summary, paraphrase and plagiarism in academic writing. Paper presented at the Symposium on Second Language Writing, Murcia, Spain, 20–22 May, 2010.

Kolich, A. (1983) Plagiarism: The worm of reason. *College English*, 45, 141–148.

Kristeva, J. (1980) *Desire in language: A semiotic approach to literature and art*. Columbia University Press, New York, NY.

Kroll, B. M. (1988) How college freshmen view plagiarism. *Written Communication*, 5, 203–221.

Larkham, P. J. and Manns, S. (2002) Plagiarism and its Treatment in Higher Education. *Journal of Further and Higher Education*, 26(4), 339–349.

Lea, M. R. and Street, B. V. (1998) Student writing in higher education: An academic literacies approach. *Studies in Higher Education*, 23, 157–172.

Leki, I. (1992) *Understanding ESL writers: A guide for teachers*. Heinemann, Portsmouth, NH.

Li, X. and Xiong, L. (1996) Chinese researchers debate rash of plagiarism cases. *Science*, 274, 337–338.

Lillis, T. M. (2001) *Student writing access, regulation, desire*. Routledge, London.

Lillis, T. (1997) New voices in academia? The regulative nature of academic writing conventions. *Language and Education*, 11, 182–199.

Liu, D. (2005) Plagiarism in ESOL students: Is cultural conditioning truly the major culprit? *ELT Journal*, 59, 234–241.

LoCastro, V. and Masuko, M. (2002) Plagiarism and academic writing of learners of English. *Hermes Journal of Linguistics*, 28, 11–33.

Love, P. G. and Simmons, J. M. (1997, November). The meaning and mediated nature of cheating and plagiarism among graduate students in a college of education. Paper presented at the meeting of the Association for the Study of Higher Education, Albuquerque, NM. (ERIC Document Reproduction Service No. ED 415 826).

Matalene, C. (1985) Contrastive rhetoric: An American writing teacher in China. *College English*, 47, 789–808.

McCabe, D. L. and Trevino, L. K. (1997) Individual and contextual influences on academic dishonesty: A multicampus investigation. *Research in Higher Education*, 38, 379–396.

McCullough, M. and Holmberg, M. (2005) Using the Google search engine to detect word-for-word plagiarism in master's theses: A preliminary study. *College Student Journal*, 39.

Moon, Y. (2002) Korean university students' awareness of plagiarism in summary writings. *Language Research*, 38(4), 1349–1365.

Nature (2012) Formatting Guide to Authors [WWW Document]. URL http://www.nature.com/nature/authors/gta/#a5.4

Norton, L. S., Tilley, A. J., Newstead, S. E. and Franklyn-Stokes, A. (2001) The pressures of assessment in undergraduate courses and their effect on student behaviours. *Assessment and Evaluation in Higher Education*, 26, 269–284.

Organisation for Economic Cooperation and Development (OECD) (2012) Foreign/international students enrolled [WWW Document]. URL http://stats.oecd.org/Index.aspx?DatasetCode=RFOREIGN

Organisation for Economic Co-operation and Development (2010) *Education at a glance: 2010 OECD indicators*. OECD Pub., Paris, France.

Park, C. (2003) In other (people's) words: Plagiarism by university students: literature and lessons. *Assessment and Evaluation in Higher Education*, 28(5), 471–488.

Pecorari, D. (2001) Plagiarism and international students: How the English-speaking university responds, in: D. Belcher and A. Hirvela (eds), *Linking literacies: Perspectives on L2 reading-writing connections*. Ann Arbor: University of Michigan Press, pp. 229–245.

Pecorari, D. (2003) Good and original: Plagiarism and patchwriting in academic second-language writing. *Journal of Second Language Writing*, 12, 317–345.

Pecorari, D. (2006) Visible and occluded citation features in postgraduate second-language writing. *English for Specific Purposes*, 25, 4–29.

Pecorari, D. (2008a) *Academic Writing and Plagiarism: A Linguistic Analysis*. Continuum, London.

Pecorari, D. (2008b) Repeated language in academic discourse: The case of biology background statements. *Nordic Journal of English Studies*, 7, 9–33.

Pecorari, D. (2008c) Plagiarism, patchwriting and source use: Best practice in the composition classroom, in: P. Friedrich (ed.), *Teaching Academic Writing*. Continuum, London, pp. 222–241.

Pecorari, D., Shaw, P., Irvine, A. and Malmström, H. (2011) English for Academic Purposes at Swedish Universities: Teachers' objectives and practices. *Ibérica*, 22, 58–78.

Pecorari, D. and Shaw, P. (2012) Types of student intertextuality and faculty attitudes. *Journal of Second Language Writing*, 21, 149–164.

Peh, W. C. G. and Arokiasamy, J. (2008) Plagiarism: A joint statement from the Singapore Medical Journal and the Medical Journal of Malaysia. *Singapore Medical Journal*, 49(12), 965–966.

Pickard, J. (2006) Staff and student attitudes to plagiarism at University College Northampton. *Assessment and Evaluation in Higher Education*, 31(2), 215–232.

Pinker, S. (1994) *The language instinct*. Penguin, London.

Porte, G. K. (1995) Writing wrongs: Copying as a strategy for underachieving EFL writers. *ELT Journal*, 49(2), 144–151.

Price, M. (2002) Beyond "Gotcha!": Situating plagiarism in policy and pedagogy. *College Composition and Communication*, 54, 88–115.

Rinnert, C. and Kobayashi, H. (2005) Borrowing words and ideas: Insights from Japanese L1 writers. *Journal of Asian Pacific Communication*, 15, 15–29.

Roig, M. (2001) Plagiarism and Paraphrasing Criteria of College and University Professors. *Ethics and Behavior*, 11, 307–323.

Rosamond, B. (2002) Plagiarism, Academic Norms and the Governance of the Profession. *Politics*, 22(3), 167–174. doi:10.1111/1467-9256.00172

Schneider, B. and Andre, J. (2005) University Preparation for Workplace Writing: Perceptions of Students in Three Disciplines. *Journal of Business Communication*, 52(2), 195–218.

Selwyn, N. (2008) 'Not necessarily a bad thing . . .': a study of online plagiarism amongst undergraduate students. *Assessment and Evaluation in Higher Education*, 33(5), 465–479.

Senders, S. (2008) Academic plagiarism and the limits of theft, in: C. Eisner and M. Vicinus (eds), *Originality, imitation and plagiarism: Teaching writing in the digital age*. University of Michigan Press, Ann Arbor, MI, pp. 195–207.

Shaw, P. and Pecorari, D. (2013). Types of intertextuality in chairman's statements. *Nordic Journal of English Studies*, 12(1), 37–68.

Shaw, P. and McMillion, A. (2008) Proficiency effects and compensation in advanced second-language reading. *Nordic Journal of English Studies*, 7(3), 123–143.

Shen, F. (1989) The classroom and the wider culture: Identity as a key to learning English composition. *College Composition and Communication*, 40: 459–466.

Sherman, J. (1992) Your own thoughts in your own words. *ELT Journal*, 46, 190–198.

Sims, R. L. (2002) The effectiveness of a plagiarism prevention policy: A longitudinal study of student views. *Teaching Business Ethics*, 6, 477–482.

Solin, A. (2004). Intertextuality as mediation: On the analysis of intertextual relations in public discourse. *Text – Interdisciplinary Journal for the Study of Discourse, 24(2), 267–296.*

Stearns, L. (1999) Copy wrong: Plagiarism, process, property and the law, in: L. Buranen and A. M. Roy (eds), *Perspectives on plagiarism and intellectual property in a postmodern world*. State University of New York Press, Albany, pp. 5–17.

Sutherland-Smith, W. (2005) Pandora's box: Academic perceptions of student plagiarism in writing. *Journal of English for Academic Purposes*, 4, 83–95.

Sutherland-Smith, W. (2008) *Plagiarism, the Internet and student learning: Improving academic integrity*. Routledge, New York.

Sutherland-Smith, W. (2010) Retribution, deterrence and reform: The dilemmas of plagiarism management in universities. *Journal of Higher Education Policy and Management*, 32, 5–16.

Sutton, A., Taylor, D. (2011) Confusion about collusion: Working together and academic integrity. *Assessment and Evaluation in Higher Education,* 36, 831–841.

Swales, J. (1990) *Genre analysis: English in academic and research settings*. Cambridge University Press, Cambridge.

Tadros, A. (1993) The pragmatics of text averral and attribution in academic texts, in: M. Hoey (ed.), *Data, description, discourse*. Harper Collins, London, pp. 98–114.

Taylor, P. and Keeter, S. (2010) *Millenials: Confident. Connected. Open to change*. Pew Research Center, Washington DC.

Thompson, G. and Ye, Y. (1991) Evaluation in the reporting verbs used in academic papers. *Applied Linguistics*, 12, 365–382.

Timm, A. (2007a) Educational practices at undergraduate level in Greece. Paper presented at the International Students, Academic Writing and Plagiarism Conference, Lancaster University, 5–7 September.

Timm, A. (2007b) Educational practices at undergraduate level in India. Paper presented at the International Students, Academic Writing and Plagiarism Conference, Lancaster University, 5–7 September.

Turnitin (2012): Products: Overview [WWW Document]. URL http://turnitin.com/en_us/products/overview

URKUND (nd) [WWW Document]. URL http://www.urkund.com/int/en/uoh.asp

Ward, J. (2001) EST: Evading scientific text. *English for Specific Purposes*, 20, 141–152.

Wheeler, G. (2009) Plagiarism in the Japanese universities: Truly a cultural matter? *Journal of Second Language Writing*, 18, 17–29.

Yeo, S. (2007) First-year university science and engineering students' understanding of plagiarism. *Higher Education Research and Development*, 26, 199–216.

Yilmaz, I. (2007) Plagiarism? No we're just borrowing better English. *Nature*, 449–658.

Subject Index

Author Index

WRITING FOR ACADEMIC JOURNALS

Third Edition

Rowena Murray

9780335263028 (Paperback)
September 2013

eBook also available

This book unravels the process of writing academic papers. It tells readers what good papers look like and how they can be written. Busy academics must develop productive writing practices quickly. No one has time for trial and error. To pass external tests of research output we must write to a high standard while juggling other professional tasks. This may mean changing our writing behaviours.

Key features:

- New material on the politics of publishing
- New material on online writing groups and the use of social media
- A new concluding chapter on next steps in reading, writing and researching including use of blogging and tweeting to increase awareness of journal articles

www.openup.co.uk

THE NEW ACADEMIC
A Strategic Handbook

Shelda Debowski

9780335245352 (Paperback)
2012

eBook also available

In today's academic environment, new and early-career academics need to operate strategically as teachers, researchers and leaders in order to establish themselves and progress in their careers. This book explores the various platforms an academic must straddle, providing practical and valuable guidance on how they might best be managed in order to achieve career success.

Key features:

- Explains the way academics are now assessed and evaluated
- Explores the key support strategies that can be accessed, including mentors and sponsors
- Practical checklists and tips on academic practices

www.openup.co.uk

 OPEN UNIVERSITY PRESS
McGraw - Hill Education